ROME TRAVEL GUIDE 2025 TO 2026

A Traveler's Guide to Hidden Rome

RAFAEL M. STONES

Copyright © [2025 by Rafael M. Stones]

All rights are reserved. No part of this publication may be reproduced, distributed, or transmitted in any form or by any means, including photocopying, recording, or other electronic or mechanical methods, without the prior written permission of the publisher, except in the case of brief quotations embodied in critical reviews and certain other noncommercial uses permitted by copyright law.

This book is a work of fiction (or nonfiction), and any resemblance to actual individuals, living or dead, or actual events is purely coincidental. The views expressed by the author are personal and do not necessarily reflect the views of the publisher.

Table of Contents

CHAPTER 1:	**8**
GETTING TO ROME	**8**
Arriving by Train	11
Reaching Rome by Road	12
Getting to Rome by Sea	13
First Moments in Rome	14
First Cultural Encounters	19
Where to Stay & Your First 24 Hours in Rome	19
Getting to Your Hotel or Apartment	22
The Ancient City vs. Modern Rome	24
CHAPTER 2:	**29**
Local Transportation & Getting Around the Eternal City	**29**
When to Walk vs. When to Ride—Sample Scenarios	36
The Basics—Rome's Three Metro Lines	37
How to Use a Bus in Rome	42
CHAPTER 3:	**53**
Neighborhoods, Hotels, and Unique Lodgings	**53**
Let's begin with the essential decision: Where in Rome should you stay?	53
Luxury Hotels	56
Mid-Range Hotels	57
Budget Hotels & Hostels	58
Booking Your Stay	61
When to Book	61
How to Book	62
CHAPTER 4:	**69**
Top Attractions in Rome	**69**
The Colosseum—Empire, Blood, and Spectacle	69
Palatine Hill	75
Farnese Gardens and Renaissance Additions	76
The Pantheon	78
Piazza Navona	83
Campo de' Fiori	88
CHAPTER 5:	**93**
VATICAN CITY	**93**
CHAPTER 6:	**108**
Vatican Museums and the Sistine Chapel	**108**
CHAPTER 7:	**116**

SHOPPING IN ROME	116
CHAPTER 8:	**121**
ROMAN NIGHTLIFE	**121**
CHAPTER 9:	**127**
ROMAN CUISINE	**127**
CHAPTER 10:	**136**
ROME FOR FAMILIES	**136**
ITINERARY	**141**
3-Day Family Itinerary with Kids	141
5-Day Family Itinerary	142
7-Day Family Itinerary:	142

INTRODUCTION

"To step into Rome is to walk into a living, breathing chronicle of civilization."
Rome—Roma, as the locals call it—is not just another destination. It is a city that carries the entire weight of Western civilization on its shoulders, and it does so with elegance, chaos, beauty, and passion. A city of paradoxes, it is at once ancient and modern, sacred and secular, regal and rebellious. Every alley, every stone, every worn marble stairway whispers stories of gods and emperors, of saints and sinners, of revolutionaries and artists.

This book opens with Rome not just as a city, but as an experience—one that reaches out across centuries to touch everyone who steps into its sun-drenched piazzas or its cool, shadowed basilicas. Whether you arrive by train through the bustling Termini Station, step off a cruise into Civitavecchia, or descend into the eternal city from the skies at Fiumicino Airport, you'll be entering more than just Italy's capital. You'll be entering one of the most important cities in the history of the world.

Why Rome Matters
Few places in the world hold as much cultural, historical, and spiritual weight as Rome. For over two thousand years, it has served as a stage for some of humanity's most significant events. It was the heart of the Roman Republic and Empire, the cradle of Christian power as the home of the Vatican, and later, a vital player in the Italian Renaissance and Baroque periods. Every generation of humankind—from ancient generals to Renaissance masters, religious pilgrims to modern tourists—has found a place within its walls.

But Rome's significance isn't confined to the past. Modern-day Rome is a dynamic metropolis, full of stylish locals, progressive art scenes, Michelin-starred restaurants, avant-garde fashion, and a uniquely Roman rhythm of life—slow and reflective in some quarters, electric and energetic in others.

This guide aims to uncover all of it.

More Than a Trip
Rome does something to you. It challenges your senses. The sight of a sunrise over the Forum, the scent of fresh espresso drifting through the morning streets, the feel of ancient stone beneath your fingertips, the flavors of Pecorino Romano melting into a perfect plate of Cacio e Pepe—these are more than experiences. They're transformations.

This city doesn't offer itself up all at once. Rome is layered, both literally and figuratively. Beneath churches are ruins. Beneath piazzas lie roads that once led emperors to glory. What looks like a simple wall may be 1,500 years old. What sounds like an ordinary church bell may be echoing through a structure older than most nations on Earth. To truly understand Rome, you have to let go of rushing. You must watch, listen, breathe, and let the rhythm of the city guide you.

A City for Everyone
Rome embraces all who come with curiosity. This book was written with all audiences in mind—solo wanderers with worn-out journals in hand, families looking for enriching adventures, couples seeking romantic escapes, and high-end travelers wanting luxury layered with authenticity.

You'll find guidance for:

Navigating Rome's layered history without overwhelm

Discovering both blockbuster attractions and little-known corners

Understanding the deep-rooted cultural behaviors and Roman etiquette

Finding food that speaks not just to your palate but to your soul

Crafting unforgettable experiences—whether you're here for two days or two weeks

Whether it's your first trip or your tenth, Rome never repeats herself. You'll always see something new, feel something different, and discover something hidden.

How This Book Will Guide You
This isn't just a list of what to see or do—this is a deeply researched, expertly crafted, and sensory-rich travel companion. Each chapter is structured not just by location or type of activity, but by atmosphere and experience. You'll uncover:

The stories behind the ruins, not just their names

The reasons why locals shop in Campo de' Fiori but relax in Testaccio

The cultural significance behind a dish, a fountain, or a fresco

Personal, historical, and anecdotal reflections that turn facts into memories

This book also includes practical help—transportation guides, budget tips, seasonal advice, safety recommendations, and language cues—all woven into a narrative that's easy to follow, engaging to read, and difficult to put down.

A Living, Breathing City
Rome is not perfect. It's loud. It's unpredictable. It's filled with contradictions—decaying grandeur beside modern glamor, bureaucracy clashing with beauty, and tourism bumping elbows with deeply local life. But that's what makes it real. That's what makes it unforgettable. It's not a movie set or a frozen monument to the past—it's alive, with a heartbeat that echoes through cobblestones and cathedral domes.

You won't just visit Rome.
You'll live it.
And after you leave, it will live in you.

CHAPTER 1:

GETTING TO ROME

Planning Your Roman Journey

Planning is an unseen but crucial step in the journey that begins before you set foot on the cobblestones of the Eternal City. This stage, often overlooked or rushed, can dramatically shape the quality, cost, comfort, and memory of your trip. In Rome, a city rich in history, contemporary culture, and nuanced complexities, careful planning at an early stage is not only advantageous but also necessary.

Define Your Travel Style

Rome can be many things to many people. Is this a luxury escape, a cultural pilgrimage, a budget backpacking adventure, or a family holiday? Knowing your goals helps shape everything else: where you stay, how long you visit, what neighborhoods you prioritize, and what form of transport is ideal.

Solo traveler? Your trip will be defined by your flexibility; hostels, short-term apartments, night trains, and walking will all play a part.

Couples? Consider romantic accommodations, quieter districts like Aventine Hill, and scenic train journeys.

Families? Proximity to parks, transit ease, and safe, central lodging are priorities.

Luxury seekers? Look for first-class flights or fast trains, airport limo pickups, and high-end stays near Via Veneto or Piazza di Spagna.

Students or budget travelers? Think buses, shared hostels, and flights into lower-cost regional airports like Ciampino.

When to Visit Rome: Seasons, Festivals, and Smart Timing

Rome is magical year-round, but it changes dramatically with the calendar. Deciding when to go affects your airfare, accommodation rates, crowd levels, daily comfort, and even how the city feels. Below is an in-depth guide to choosing your ideal season.

Spring (March–May)

Rome awakens with wildflowers, blossoming orange trees, and soft sunshine. Outdoor cafés reopen, locals return to the piazzas, and temperatures range from 14°C to 24°C. Holy Week and Easter are major religious events, drawing large crowds.

Pros: Comfortable weather, cultural events, vibrant city parks.
Cons: Easter week can be crowded and expensive.

Summer (June–August)
Anticipate lengthy days with plenty of sunshine (30°C+), a vibrant nightlife, and extended museum hours. Romans often leave in August, especially during Ferragosto, making some neighborhoods quieter—but still hot.

Pros: Summer festivals, music events, open-air cinemas.
Cons: High heat, high prices, tourist saturation, closed shops mid-August.

Autumn (September–November)
Golden sunsets, grape harvests, and a more relaxed pace return. September is still busy, but by October, tourism is thin. Rain increases slightly, but so does cultural depth.

Pros: Pleasant climate, food festivals, less crowded.
Cons: Occasional rain and shorter days by November.

Winter (December–February)
The most underrated season. Fewer tourists, cheaper rates, and a romantic atmosphere—especially during Christmas and New Year. Rome rarely sees snow, and temperatures remain between 4°C and 13°C.

Pros: Low costs, quiet streets, lit-up churches, and festive markets.
Cons: Some attractions have shorter hours; chilly rain is common.

Entry Requirements: Visas, Travel Documents, and Formalities
Rome, as the capital of Italy, follows the Schengen Zone rules for international arrivals.

For EU/EEA/Swiss Citizens:
No visa required.

National ID or passport valid for the stay.

No arrival/departure cards or customs declaration needed.

For the US, Canada, the UK, Australia, Japan, etc.:
Stays under 90 days:No visa, but ETIAS authorization (from 2025) is required.

After departure, the passport must be valid for at least three months.

Proof of return ticket and accommodation may be requested.

For Non-Visa-Exempt Countries:
A Schengen visa is mandatory.

Apply through the Italian consulate/embassy in your home country.

Allow at least 15–30 days for approval.

Important Notes:

Italy is very strict on passport validity and overstay penalties.

ETIAS (EU Travel Information and Authorization System) will be mandatory soon for most non-EU travelers.

Budgeting Your Trip to Rome
How much does it cost to get to Rome? It depends entirely on where you're coming from, how early you book, and what kind of experience you're after.

Type of Traveler   Daily Budget (excl. flights)
Backpacker: €50–€70
Mid-range tourist: €100–€180
Luxury traveler: €250–€600+

Flights from major regions (avg round-trip if booked 3–4 months ahead):

New York to Rome (FCO)—$550–$900 economy

London to Rome—€50–€200(budget airlines to full service)

Sydney to Rome – AUD $1,300–$2,000

Lagos to Rome – ₦500,000–₦1,200,000 (check visa packages too)

Booking tips, how to use flight comparison tools, shoulder season discounts, and regional airports will be discussed in detail shortly.

Arriving by Train

Rome is a major node in Italy's extensive high-speed rail network and offers connections from cities across the country and the continent. Traveling by train is not only comfortable and scenic but also often faster than flying for many regional trips.

Rome's Main Train Stations
Roma Termini: Central hub, busiest station in Italy, connections to metro lines A & B.

Roma Tiburtina: A modern hub for high-speed trains like Italo, located slightly east of the center.

Roma Ostiense: Serves some regional trains and connections to Fiumicino via FL1.

High-Speed Trains (Frecciarossa, Frecciargento, Italo):
From Florence: 1h 30m

From Milan: 3h

From Naples: 1h 10m

From Venice: 3h 45m

International Trains:
Paris to Rome: Via Milan, ~10 hours total

Munich to Rome: ~12 hours, with changes

Zurich to Rome: ~8 hours

Overnight trains are also available on select routes.

Booking Tips:
Use the websites or applications for Italo (private high-speed train) or Trenitalia (state railway).

Booking early can reduce prices dramatically—discounts of up to 70%.

Trains are clean, punctual, and often luxurious in first class.

Lockers, food courts, pharmacies, and tourist information desks can be found at Rome's rail stations.

Reaching Rome by Road

If you're traveling through Italy or Southern Europe by road, Rome is well-connected by a ring of motorways and national roads.

By Bus: Budget-Friendly and Expansive
Major Bus Companies:

FlixBus

Itabus

MarinoBus

Bus Center

Most long-distance buses arrive at Tiburtina Station or Rome Anagnina.

Tickets are very cheap (as low as €5–€30), but travel times are longer.

Modern buses offer Wi-Fi, USB ports, bathrooms, and reclining seats.

Examples
Naples to Rome: 2–2.5 hrs

Florence to Rome: 3.5 hrs

Paris to Rome: 20–22 hrs

Bucharest to Rome: 30 hrs+

By Car: Driving into the Eternal City
Rome is accessible via A1 (Autostrada del Sole), the country's main north-south artery.

Other major roads:

A24 from L'Aquila and the Adriatic coast

SS1 Via Aurelia from the west coast

GRA (Grande Raccordo Anulare)—Rome's beltway

Cautions:
Driving in Rome is not recommended for visitors.

ZTL (Zona Traffico Limitato) restricts driving in central areas without a permit—hefty fines apply.

Parking is scarce and expensive near major landmarks.

When to Consider Driving:
Visiting rural Lazio towns before Rome.

Road-tripping across Tuscany or Umbria.

Staying in suburban villas or agriturismos.

Getting to Rome by Sea

Despite not being close to the ocean, Rome can reach its seaport in Civitavecchia, which is around 80 kilometers (50 miles) northwest of the city. If you're arriving via cruise ship or ferry from Sardinia, Spain, or the south of France, this is your entry.

From Civitavecchia to Rome:
Regional Train: Civitavecchia to Roma Termini in ~1h 20m

Cruise Shuttle + Train: Many cruise lines offer combined port transfers

Private Transfer/Taxi: ~€120–€150

Major Cruise Lines That Stop at Rome:
MSC Cruises

Royal Caribbean

Norwegian

Celebrity Cruises

Costa Cruises

Ferry Lines
Tirrenia, Grimaldi Lines (from Sardinia, Sicily, Barcelona, Toulon, Tunis)

Tips:
The Civitavecchia port is busy—allowing time to navigate from ship to station.

Combine your cruise with a Rome city stay before or after for a complete experience.

First Moments in Rome

"The journey to Rome doesn't end at the border—it begins there."
Your first few hours in Rome can define the rhythm of your stay. Rome doesn't greet visitors with sterile efficiency. Instead, it offers a warm, sometimes chaotic, fully sensory welcome—ancient ruins looming beside modern highways, espresso machines hissing at train stations, impatient cab drivers shouting in melodious Italian, and the distant tolling of church bells. This is not a city that eases you in gently—it pulls you in, alive and unapologetic.

Let's walk through, in detailed steps, exactly what to expect from the moment you arrive to your first breath of Roman air.

Airport Arrival
A. Immigration and Customs
If you arrive by air, particularly at Fiumicino (FCO) or Ciampino (CIA), your first stop will be passport control. Rome's immigration process varies depending on nationality and time of day.

EU/Schengen Travelers:

Use the eGates for biometric passports—often a quick process.

No customs declarations are needed unless carrying restricted goods.

Non-EU Travelers:

Queue for immigration stamp; officers may ask:

Where you're staying (have hotel address or Airbnb printout).

Return ticket details.

Proof of sufficient funds (rare, but possible).

Average wait time: 15–45 minutes, longer in peak seasons.

Baggage Claim & Customs:

Signs in Italian and English.

Free luggage carts are available.

Customs inspections are rare unless declared items or dogs are triggered.

First Impressions:

Fiumicino's arrivals hall is modern, with tourist booths, SIM card vendors, and cafes.

Don't expect airport staff to speak perfect English, but most are helpful.

You're in Italy now—the pace is relaxed, smiles are genuine, but things may take time.

Train Arrival
Arriving by rail—especially on a Frecciarossa or Italo high-speed train—is one of the most seamless entries into Rome.

Roma Termini Station—More than a Terminal
Massive and historic, yet modernized.

Platforms 1–29 are clearly labeled, with elevators/escalators to the main concourse.

Services include:

Baggage storage (€6 for 5 hours at KiPoint)

Pharmacies, cafés, a full supermarket

Metro Lines A and B below ground

Rome Tourist Info Center (near Platform 24)

A little distance outside Piazza dei Cinquecento are taxi ranks and shuttle stops.

Watch out for:
Pickpockets—especially at crowded escalators and ticket machines.

"Helpers" who insist on assisting with tickets and then demand tips.

Use official Trenitalia/Italo ticket booths or machines with English options.

Port Arrival
Cruise travelers docking at Civitavecchia must factor in the one- to two-hour journey into Rome.

Disembarkation starts early—allowing lines, security, and shuttle transfers.

Best option: Direct regional train (frequent, affordable, ~€5–€10).

A Roma Day Pass (BIRG) can be purchased at the station and includes return fare and unlimited Rome transport.

The port area is industrial—don't linger unless staying overnight.

Local Transport
Rome's streets, though chaotic at first glance, follow an ancient rhythm. Learning how to get around efficiently saves you time and nerves. Here's a complete orientation to Rome's public transport system:

The Metro (Subway)
Rome has 3 main metro lines:

Line A (Orange): Key stops include Termini, Spagna (Spanish Steps), and Ottaviano (Vatican).

Line B (Blue): Connects Colosseum, Termini, and EUR district.

Line C (Green): Less central, expanding toward suburbs and archaeological sites.

Tickets:

Standard ticket (BIT)—€1.50, valid for 100 minutes, includes one metro ride + bus/tram.

24, 48, 72-hour and weekly passes are available.

Tickets sold at:

Metro vending machines (multiple languages)

Tabacchi shops (look for the white "T")

Newsstands and some hotel desks

Pro Tips:

Validate paper tickets before boarding (machines at station entrances).

Metro closes around 11:30 PM (1:30 AM on weekends).

Buses and Trams
Rome's bus network is vast and often confusing for newcomers.

Use Google Maps, Rome2Rio, or ATAC (Rome's official transit app).

Buses are numbered; signs list stops and routes.

Some lines operate 24/7 (night buses with an "N" prefix).

Trams are slower but scenic—useful for outer neighborhoods.

Taxis
Use only official white taxis with a roof sign and license number.

Flag one down or go to a taxi stand (you can't hail from the street randomly).

Starting fare: ~€4; surcharge for night/weekend/airport rides.

Apps like FreeNow (Europe's Uber-like taxi app) work reliably.

Avoid scams: Insist on the meter, or agree on a price before entering.

Ride-Sharing
Only the luxury categories (Uber Black, Lux) are available on Uber.

Locals often use ItTaxi or MyTaxi.

Rome is more taxi-oriented than ride-sharing—plan accordingly.

Walking
Rome is a pedestrian's paradise.

Many of the most beautiful parts of the city—Trastevere, the Forum, Vatican alleys—are walkable.

Wear very comfortable shoes—cobblestones are charming but brutal.

Expect hills, uneven terrain, and sudden steps.

Getting Connected: SIM Cards, Wi-Fi, and Navigation
The Eternal City might be ancient, but it's digitally connected.

Mobile SIMs
Vendors like TIM, Vodafone, and WindTre offer tourist SIM packages.

Available at airports, Termini, and major shops.

~€20 gets you ~20–50 GB + some international calls/texts.

Must show passport for activation.

eSIMs
Ideal for modern phones.

Providers like Airalo, Holafly, or Ubigi offer instant setup.

Wi-Fi
Free Wi-Fi in most major piazzas, hotels, and cafés.

Not always reliable in open-air areas—better to have mobile data.

Essential Apps:
ATAC Roma – local transport schedules

Rome2Rio—route planner for events and modes

Google Translate – Italian signage & menus

Visit Rome Official Apps for Eve events and ticket booking

First Cultural Encounters

Language: Italian is the norm; English is spoken at hotels, tourist spots, and by younger locals.

Gestures: Italians speak with their hands—don't be intimidated.

Pace: Fast in traffic, slow at meals. Accept this duality.

Customer Service: Polite, but don't expect American-style cheeriness.

Currency: Euro (€); cards accepted widely, but carry cash for cafés, taxis, and markets.

Where to Stay & Your First 24 Hours in Rome

"Don't expect to see Rome in a day; it wasn't built in one."

You've made it to the Eternal City. Whether you arrived by air, rail, or ship, your senses are likely overwhelmed. The scent of roasting coffee beans. The echo of Vespa engines. Ancient ruins peeking out between Renaissance palaces. The weight of 2,000 years of civilization surrounds you—but before you lose yourself in the wonders, you need to ground yourself. That means finding the right place to stay and knowing how to spend your first 24 hours wisely, without rushing.

Choosing Where to Stay
Rome is not a small, one-center "downtown" city. Instead, it's a mosaic of neighborhoods—each with its own mood, rhythm, and advantages. Choosing where to

stay should match your travel purpose, lifestyle, budget, and personal tastes. Let's explore some of the main districts:

A. Centro Storico (Historic Center)
Best for: First-time visitors, luxury lovers, romantic travelers

Piazza Navona, the Pantheon, and Campo de' Fiori are just a few of the famous sights in the center of ancient Rome. This district places you within walking distance of major attractions.

Accommodation: Mostly boutique hotels, historic inns, and Airbnbs in 16th–18th century buildings.

Vibe: Romantic, elegant, and atmospheric—but expect crowds and higher prices.

Drawbacks: Limited nightlife after 11 PM, touristy restaurants, expensive lodging.

Suggested streets include Piazza Farnese (sophisticated), Via dei Coronari (antiques), and Via Giulia (calm, attractive).

B. Trastevere
Best for: Bohemians, couples, food lovers, photographers

Just across the Tiber River, this former working-class district offers cobbled lanes, ivy-covered walls, candlelit trattorias, and artisan shops.

Accommodation: Trendy guesthouses, mid-range hotels, and B&Bs.

Vibe: Youthful yet rooted in tradition; Rome's nightlife heart after sunset.

Drawbacks: No metro access, uneven cobblestones, some noise at night.

Highlights: Piazza Santa Maria in Trastevere, Villa Farnesina, Janiculum Hill views

C. Monti
Best for: Hip travelers, solo tourists, creatives

Tucked between the Colosseum and Termini Station, Monti feels like a village within the city. Fashion boutiques, organic wine bars, and indie galleries line its hilly streets.

Accommodation: Stylish B&Bs, apartments, and cool hotels like The Fifteen Keys or Nerva.

Vibe: Trendy without being touristy. Ideal for photographers and foodies.

Drawbacks: Hilly terrain, some limited transport options.

Streets to explore: Via Urbana, Via Panisperna, Piazza della Madonna dei Monti

D. Prati / Vatican Area
Best for: Religious pilgrims, families, longer stays

Home to the Vatican Museums and St. Peter's Basilica, Prati is elegant, quieter, and slightly removed from Rome's chaotic core.

Accommodation: Business hotels, large apartments, and mid-range stays.

Vibe: More local, wide boulevards, excellent shopping (Via Cola di Rienzo).

Drawbacks: Slightly further from Rome's ancient center, but clean and walkable.

Bonus: Well-connected via Metro Line A and buses

E. Testaccio
Best for: Culinary tourists, cultural travelers, those wanting authenticity

A less-touristed gem southeast of the Aventine Hill, Testaccio is where Romans go to eat — and live.

Accommodation: Affordable guesthouses, modern rentals, and family-run lodgings.
—and
Vibe: Gritty-chic, full of life, home to Rome's best food market and authentic trattorias.

Drawbacks: Limited landmarks nearby, but easy access to Trastevere and Aventine.

Must-visit: Mercato Testaccio, Non-Catholic Cemetery, Monte dei Cocci

F. Termini / Esquilino
Best for: Budget travelers, backpackers, transport hubs

Convenient for early departures and arrivals, but not the most charming area. Still, some gems exist here.

Accommodation: Budget hotels, hostels, and international chains.

Vibe: Mixed—diverse, chaotic, but practical.

Drawbacks: Can feel gritty; avoid dimly lit streets at night.

Booking Tips: Hotels vs. Apartments vs. B&Bs
Rome has over 3,000 registered accommodations. Your choice matters—not just for budget, but for experience.

Hotels
3-star: Clean, central, ~€100–€150 per night.

4-star: Often boutique style, some with rooftop terraces.

5-star: Palatial. Think Hotel de Russie, Hassler Roma, and J.K. Place Roma.

Apartments (Airbnb, VRBO)
More space, kitchens, and local feel.

Great for families or week-long stays.

Watch for stairs (no elevators in old buildings), and double-check A/C and Wi-Fi.

B&Bs
Cozy, family-run, and often breakfast-included.

Ask about check-in hours and luggage storage.

Getting to Your Hotel or Apartment

Once you've arrived in Rome, how you get to your accommodation matters—not just for ease, but for cost and first impressions.

Airport to Hotel
Taxi: Flat rate from Fiumicino (€50) and Ciampino (€31) to central Rome—official taxis only!

Private Transfers: Pre-booked for comfort and reliability.

Leonardo Express Train: Direct to Termini in 32 minutes (€14).

Terravision Shuttle: Budget-friendly to Termini (€6–€7).

Train Station to Hotel
Walk, take a taxi, or take the Metro if staying nearby.

For Centro Storico or Trastevere, taxis are easiest with luggage.

Your First 24 Hours in Rome
Avoid the temptation to do too much. You're tired. Rome isn't a checklist—it's a slow-drip espresso. Here's a curated guide to your ideal first 24 hours.

Hours 1–2: Arrive, Settle In, Freshen Up
Unpack lightly.

Charge phone, set up SIM/data.

Grab a map or download offline GPS (like Maps.me).

Hours 3–4: Take a Slow Stroll
Walk from your accommodation to a nearby piazza, gelateria, or terrace.

If in Trastevere: Stroll to Piazza Santa Maria and listen to street musicians.

If near the Pantheon: Wander to Piazza Navona, and grab espresso at Sant'Eustachio.

Hours 5–6: Early Dinner
Romans eat late—but your body may want food early.

Keep it simple: Pizza al taglio, cacio e pepe pasta, and a glass of wine.

Avoid restaurants with photo menus and staff pulling you in.

Hours 7–8: Evening Walk or Light Tour
See Rome lit up at night. There are no crowds, the air is cool, and there is magic all around.

Trevi Fountain by moonlight.

Spanish Steps with gelato.

Piazza Venezia glowing under floodlights.

Rest & Reset
Sleep well.

The Ancient City vs. Modern Rome

"Rome is not one city—it is many cities stacked atop one another, stitched together by cobblestones, memory, and light."

To appreciate Rome, you must understand that it is not organized like a modern metropolis. Instead, it's a palimpsest—a city built, destroyed, and rebuilt over and over again for more than 2,500 years. The ancient and the contemporary live side by side. A luxury boutique stands beside a medieval bell tower. A 20th-century tram rumbles past a 1st-century temple. Understanding Rome's layout—physically, historically, and culturally—is essential for making sense of what you see and how to move through it.

Rome's Historical Layers

Let's begin by breaking down the four major "eras" of Rome that influence its current geography. Every district in Rome contains traces of at least one of these layers:

A. Ancient Rome (753 BCE – 476 CE)

This is the Rome of emperors, gladiators, aqueducts, and temples.

Where to find it:

The Roman Forum: Political and religious heart of Ancient Rome.

The Colosseum: Gladiatorial arena and symbol of imperial grandeur.

Palatine Hill: Legendary birthplace of the city; home to imperial palaces.

Pantheon: Still standing, still majestic—a perfect Roman dome.

Appian Way (Via Appia Antica): Rome's oldest road, lined with tombs and catacombs.

The Baths of Caracalla and Trajan's Market: Roman engineering at its peak.

Visual cues: Ruins, arches, marble fragments, Latin inscriptions, worn travertine steps, open-air excavations.

Urban Feel: Sparse, monumental, sun-bleached. Often fenced off or open to guided visits.

B. Medieval Rome (5th – 14th Century CE)
After the empire fell, Rome became a medieval city-state, governed by popes and feuding noble families.

Where to find it:

Trastevere: Labyrinthine alleys, small squares, artisan shops.

Campo de' Fiori & Via Giulia: Once lawless, now elegant.

Jewish Ghetto: Europe's oldest continuous Jewish community.

Torre delle Milizie & Torre Argentina: Bell towers and ruins.

Visual cues: Narrow streets, uneven paving stones, churches with plain façades and ornate interiors, towers rising unpredictably among houses.
interiors, and
Urban interiors are animate, atmospheric, and slightly shadowy—like stepping into a Caravaggio painting.

C. Renaissance & Baroque Rome (15th–18th Century CE)
This is the Rome of Michelangelo, Bernini, and Caravaggio, where the papacy rebuilt Rome as a capital of Christian power and art.

Where to find it:

Piazza Navona: Built on a Roman stadium, now adorned with Baroque fountains.

St. Peter's Basilica & Vatican Museums: The pinnacle of ecclesiastical art.

Churches like Sant'Agnese in Agone, San Luigi dei Francesi, Il Gesù

Fountains: Trevi Fountain, Fontana del Tritone

Visual cues: Marble facades, grand piazzas, fountains, spiral columns, optical illusions in architecture, and churches hidden behind modest doors.

Urban Feel: Ornate, theatrical, spiritual. A walk through papal power and artistic grandeur.

D. Modern Rome (19th Century–Present Day)

After becoming the capital of unified Italy in 1871, Rome began its transformation into a modern state capital. Today, you'll find government ministries, embassies, museums, universities, trendy cafés, and gritty suburbs.

Where to find it:

Termini and Esquilino: Rail hub and multicultural gateway.

Prati: Rationalist grid planning, elegant facades.

EUR District: Mussolini's surreal Fascist-era vision of modernity.

Monti, Testaccio, and San Lorenzo: urban villages alive with youth culture and nightlife.

Visual cues: Tree-lined boulevards, uniform architecture, modern art museums, street art, and international cuisine.

Urban Feel: Functional, dynamic, often underrated. This is where many Romans live, study, and work.

Rome's Geographical Structure

Rome's topography shaped its history—and still defines its neighborhoods. Originally founded on seven hills, the city has since sprawled far beyond them, but their names remain important markers.

The Seven Hills of Rome:

Palatine Hill—Where Romulus founded Rome; today a serene archaeological park.

Capitoline Hill—Once sacred, now home to Michelangelo's piazza and museums.

Aventine Hill—elegant and leafy, with secret gardens and the famous keyhole view.

Caelian Hill—Quiet, dotted with ancient churches and villas.

Esquiline Hill—Large and diverse; home to Santa Maria Maggiore.

Viminal Hill—Near Termini; home to Rome's opera house and ministries.

Quirinal Hill—Seat of the Italian President; high-end hotels and palazzi.

These hills are not just historical—they impact how you explore Rome:

Walking between them often means stairs, slopes, and panoramic views.

Districts are loosely anchored around them.

Ancient roads radiated outward from these points.

Rome's Official Districts (Rioni)
The central part of Rome is divided into 22 ""Rioni"—ancient administrative zones still used in modern mapping.

Here are a few important ones to know as a visitor:

Rione	Name	Highlights
I	Monti	Colosseum, boutique shops, bohemian cafés
II.		Trevi Fountain, Quirinale Palace
VI	Parione	Piazza Navona, Via del Governo Vecchio
VII	Regola	Campo de' Fiori, Tiber River views
XIII	Trastevere	Santa Maria, nightlife, artisans
XV	Esquilino	Termini Station, multicultural markets
XXII	Prati	Vatican, wide boulevards, upscale shops

Why this matters:
Knowing your region helps you orient yourself. For example, if your accommodation is listed as "Rione I – Monti," you'll know to expect cobbled lanes, cool shops, and easy access to the Forum and Colosseum.

How to Think Like a Roman When Navigating

Tourists get lost in Rome not just because streets are winding but because they expect modern logic from an ancient layout. Here's how to adapt:

Landmarks Over Street Names
Romans give directions using monuments, piazzas, and fountains—not addresses.

"Go past the church, turn left at the gelateria, and look for the obelisk" is common.

Piazzas Are Anchors
Treat Rome's piazzas as mental "stations." Learn them like a subway map.

Examples

Piazza Venezia: Central hub, access to Via del Corso, the Forum, and Capitoline Hill.

Piazza del Popolo: Northern entrance to the city and park access.

Campo de' Fiori: Market by day, nightlife by night.

Tiber River = Natural Compass
The river curves through the city—learning its bends helps you understand where you are.

East Bank: Historic center, Colosseum, Termini.

West Bank: Trastevere, Vatican, Gianicolo Hill.

Walking Rome
Rome is a walking city, but not like Paris or New York. Here's what to expect:

Streets change names constantly. A single road may have three names in 500 meters.

Sidewalks are inconsistent. Some sidewalks vanish entirely, so if necessary, walk confidently in the road.

Everything is closer than it looks. A 30-minute walk often takes 90 minutes because you'll stop for art, coffee, photos, and piazzas.

CHAPTER 2:

Local Transportation & Getting Around the Eternal City

Understanding Rome's Layout
Before you hop onto a metro, flag down a taxi, or rent a Vespa, you must understand something fundamental: Rome is not a grid. Rome is a living museum, layered in centuries of architecture, history, and chaos.

To move confidently through it, whether for a three-day visit or a month-long stay, you need to first comprehend its physical and cultural layout. This is not just about maps—it's about rhythm, perception, and atmosphere. Understanding Rome's neighborhoods (called rioni) and their distinctive personalities is your first step to moving through the city like a Roman.

The Core of the City—The Historic Center (Centro Storico)
The Centro Storico is the beating heart of Rome. It's what people imagine when they dream of cobblestone streets, baroque fountains, crumbling ruins tucked between cafes, and tiny alleys leading to breathtaking piazzas.

Key Landmarks in the Centro Storico:

The Pantheon

Piazza Navona

Campo de' Fiori

Trevi Fountain

Spanish Steps

This area is ideal for walking. Cars are restricted, and most streets are pedestrian-friendly but winding and narrow. It's not unusual to turn a corner and stumble into a Roman column, a 16th-century church, or an open-air market.

Navigation Tips

Streets are poorly marked and irregular. Don't rely on North-South orientation.

Use landmarks, not addresses: "Near the Pantheon" is more effective than a street name.

Google Maps works, but a paper map is helpful for the Centro Storico's disjointed streets.

The Vatican Area (Borgo and Prati Districts)
Although technically a separate country, Vatican City is embedded within Rome and surrounded by the neighborhoods of Borgo and Prati. These areas are elegant, spacious, and more organized than the Centro Storico.

Features:

Prati has wide boulevards and is ideal for shopping and staying in quieter hotels.

Borgo has historic streets and religious institutions.

Excellent Metro access via Ottaviano and Cipro stations.

This area is highly walkable and well-connected, though crowd control during major papal events (e.g., Easter) can affect transport.

Trastevere—The Bohemian Soul of Rome
Across the Tiber River lies Trastevere, Rome's artsy, romantic, and ancient neighborhood known for:

Narrow lanes

Ivy-covered facades

Late-night eateries and wine bars

Walking is the only real option here—no metro stations, and very few streets can accommodate cars. Trastevere feels like a village within the city, ideal for evening strolls.

Testaccio—Local, More Gritty, and Authentic

South of the Aventine, Testaccio is a district with a strong working-class heritage and a vibrant food culture. While fewer tourists venture here, the area is gaining popularity.

Highlights:

Authentic Roman cuisine

Monte Testaccio (ancient hill of broken amphorae)

MACRO Museum of Contemporary Art

Public transport is fairly accessible via bus and tram, though metro service is limited.

Termini & Esquilino – Transportation Hub & Multicultural Vibe

Rome's Termini Station is the city's main transportation nerve center. Surrounding it is Esquilino, a diverse, sometimes gritty, yet fascinating district.

Features:

Main hub for trains, airport buses, and two metro lines (A & B)

Hotels are plentiful and affordable

Nearby landmarks: Santa Maria Maggiore, Piazza della Repubblica

While the area is functional and affordable, it's not the most romantic part of Rome — more ideal for convenience than ambiance.

Monti – The Trendy, Ancient Hotspot

Situated between the Colosseum and Termini, Monti is a delightful blend of bohemian flair and ancient ruins. It's Rome's answer to Brooklyn or Shoreditch.

Great for boutique shopping

Hidden wine bars and vintage shops

Walkable to many key sites

Monti combines convenience with charm and has excellent metro access via Cavour Station.

San Lorenzo – The Student Zone
Just east of Termini is San Lorenzo, a youthful, gritty, and rebellious district known for street art and nightlife.

Ideal for younger travelers, backpackers

Home to La Sapienza University

Limited public transport; best accessed by tram or bus

EUR & Southern Rome – Fascist Architecture & Business Centers
EUR (Esposizione Universale Roma) was built under Mussolini and features wide boulevards, stark architecture, and modern museums.

Rome's financial district

Well connected via Metro Line B

Houses Museum of Roman Civilization, Palazzo della Civiltà Italiana

Not ideal for walking, but easy to reach for architecture fans or business travelers.

Roman Bridges & the Tiber River's Role in Navigation
The Tiber River (Tevere) cuts through the city and is both a guide and a barrier. While it's beautiful, it also affects how transportation lines run.

Key Bridges:

Ponte Sisto—pedestrian only, connects Trastevere to Campo de' Fiori
—pedestrian
Ponte Sant'Angelo – leads directly to the Vatican

Ponte Garibaldi—popular for sunset walks

Use the bridges as waypoints when orienting yourself. The river bends dramatically through the city, so always verify your direction—it's easy to end up on the wrong side.

Should You Walk or Ride?

Rome is often called an open-air museum, and there's no exaggeration in that metaphor. The experience of walking down a narrow cobblestone lane and turning into a sun-soaked piazza framed by centuries-old architecture is something you simply can't replicate through a bus window or from the back seat of a taxi. That said, Rome's sprawling layout, unpredictable traffic, and ancient infrastructure also pose real challenges, particularly when you're balancing time, energy, or accessibility.

This section dives into the realities, myths, and best practices of navigating Rome by foot and vehicle—breaking down who should walk, when to ride, and how to make smart decisions depending on your goals, travel style, budget, and stamina.

Walking in Rome—A Sensory Experience Like No Other

Walking in Rome isn't just a way to get from point A to point B—it is often the highlight of the trip itself. You'll walk past:

Fountains where locals refill their water bottles (called nasoni)

Streets echoing with musicians and church bells

Balconies blooming with geraniums

Layers of history underfoot—from cobblestones to ancient Roman pavement (basoli)

Best Areas for Walking:

Centro Storico (Pantheon, Trevi Fountain, Piazza Navona)

Trastevere (especially early mornings or after sunset)

Jewish Ghetto & Teatro Marcello

Via del Corso to the Spanish Steps

Roman Forum & Palatine Hill (walking path only)

Advantages:

Total immersion in sights, sounds, and smells

Discover places no map will show—like hidden courtyards or artisan shops

Avoid traffic snarls and bus delays

Burn off all that gelato and pasta

Disadvantages

Exhaustion is real:Expect to walk 10,000–20,000 steps a day as a tourist

Uneven terrain: Cobblestones can be hard on knees, ankles, and stroller wheels

Summer heat: From June to August, daytime temps can reach 35°C (95°F)

Poor signage: It's easy to get lost—carry a map or GPS-enabled device

Pro Tip:
Rome is not wheelchair- or stroller-friendly in many areas. If you or someone in your group has mobility challenges, choose accommodation near metro-accessible zones or more modern neighborhoods like Prati, Testaccio, or around Termini.

When Walking Becomes a Burden
Even the most ambitious travelers reach a point where walking becomes unsustainable. The following are warning signs that it's time to switch from foot to ride:

Midday fatigue: Between 1 pm and 4 pm, the heat and light can be punishing.

Long-distance routes: From Vatican City to the Colosseum is about 4.5 km—a 55-minute walk without stops.

Nightfall in unfamiliar neighborhoods

Inclement weather

Mobility limitations (temporary or permanent)

Tight scheduling: If you've booked back-to-back tours, riding is more efficient.

Pros & Cons of Vehicular Movement

Types of Vehicular Transport:

Metro (subway)

Bus & tram

Taxi & private hire

Electric scooters or e-bikes

Car rental

Vespa (for experienced riders only)

Key Considerations:

	Walking	Vehicle
Cost	-free	varies (from €1.50 metro ticket to €60/day scooter rental)
Access to hidden gems	Excellent	Poor
Speed across the city.	Slow	Faster
Physical demand:	high	low
Traffic risk:	None	High
Cultural immersion:	complete	limited
Environmental impact.	None	Varies
Night safety.	Good in crowds	Better in isolated areas

Conclusion:

Mixing walking and riding is the wisest approach. Plan your walking routes to include concentrated areas with high tourist density, then ride between major zones like the Vatican, Trastevere, and the Colosseum district.

Safety Tips for Walking in Rome

Be alert at crossings: Even where there's a zebra crossing (strisce pedonali), Roman drivers may not stop unless you assertively but cautiously step out.

Watch your bags: Pickpockets are discreet and fast, especially in crowds or near Termini Station.

Avoid empty alleys at night: Rome is generally safe, but stay in well-lit areas.

Wear the right shoes: Sneakers or supportive sandals with grip are essential. Leave heels or thin-soled fashion shoes at home.

When to Walk vs. When to Ride—Sample Scenarios
Scenario A: Solo Traveler on a Budget

Walk from Trastevere to Campo de' Fiori in the morning

Take Metro Line A from Spagna to Ottaviano for Vatican afternoon tour

Walk back down Via Cola di Rienzo and cross Ponte Sant'Angelo

Scenario B: Family with Children

Walk around Piazza Navona and Pantheon in the morning

Take a taxi to the Colosseum (to avoid tired little legs)

Ride the Metro from Colosseo to Cipro (Line B to A switch at Termini) for dinner in Prati

Scenario C: Luxury Traveler Staying at Hassler Roma

Private transfer or taxi between sites

Light walking tours in mornings or evenings

Hotel arranges chauffeured Vespa tour for scenic photo ops
The hotel
Scenario D: History Buff

Walking tour of Roman Forum, Palatine Hill, and Colosseum in one loop

Break for lunch in Monti, then bus to Baths of Caracalla

Evening tram to Trastevere for a wine tasting experience

How to Optimize Walking and Riding
Plan your route in zones, grouping sites by proximity (e.g., Vatican Museums, St. Peter's, and Castel Sant'Angelo in one day)

Use apps like Citymapper or Moovit to get real-time transit data

Don't rely only on Google Maps walking estimates—they don't account for Roman crowds or terrain

Carry small change and your Roma Pass or Metro ticket to avoid delays

Stop frequently for espresso, water, or gelato—these are not just snacks; they're Italian survival rituals

The Metro System—Fast but Limited

Rome's Metropolitana, or metro system, is often praised for being fast and efficient—and rightly so—but it's also known for being relatively small and underdeveloped for a capital of its size. This is due to the city's ancient infrastructure: every time someone tries to dig underground, they risk uncovering ruins from 2,000 years ago, halting construction for years. As a result, the metro remains a partial solution to city navigation—a tool, not a full strategy.

This section offers in-depth coverage of how the metro works, when to use it, how to stay safe, and why its limitations must be understood if you're going to make the most of your time in Rome.

The Basics—Rome's Three Metro Lines

Rome has only three metro lines:

Line A (Orange): Runs southeast to northwest

Line B (Blue): Runs northeast to southwest

Line C (Green): Newest line, still being expanded, not connected to Lines A or B directly (you must switch via buses or walk)

There is no "Line D" — a planned fourth line has been indefinitely delayed.

Line A—The Tourist Line
Runs from Battistini (west) to Anagnina (southeast)

Serves Vatican Museums, Piazza di Spagna (Spanish Steps), Trevi Fountain (via Barberini station), and Termini (central hub)

Stops at: Cipro, Ottaviano, Lepanto, Flaminio, Spagna, Barberini, Repubblica, Termini, Manzoni, San Giovanni, and beyond

Pros:

Very useful for visitors staying in Prati, Piazza di Spagna, or near the Vatican

Fast and fairly clean

Well-connected to key sights

Cons:

Extremely crowded during rush hours (7:30–9:30 am, 5:00–7:00 pm)

Pickpockets are active—particularly at Spagna, Termini, and Barberini

Line B—The Historical Spine
Runs from Rebibbia or Jonio (north) to Laurentina (south)

Key tourist stations: Colosseo (Colosseum), Cavour (Monti District), Circo Massimo, Piramide

It also connects to EUR, the fascist-era business district, and Ostiense train station

Pros:

Stops directly at Colosseum

Great for reaching Testaccio, Ostiense, and business centers

Intersects Line A at Termini, allowing transfers

Cons:

Some parts (especially south of Piramide) are far from tourist sights

Colosseo Station can get overwhelmed by crowds and street vendors

Line C—The Modern but Isolated Line
Runs from Monte Compatri–Pantano to San Giovanni

Eventually planned to reach Piazza Venezia (near the Roman Forum), but construction is still in progress

Pros:

Ultra-modern trains with air conditioning and automated driving

Lightly used—fewer crowds

Cons:

Not connected to other metro lines at most points (except San Giovanni on Line A)

Not useful for most tourists unless staying on the far eastern edge of Rome

Tickets, Passes, and Pricing
Rome's metro system is integrated with other public transport (bus, tram, and suburban train), and they all use the same ticketing system, known as ATAC.

Ticket Types (as of latest update):
Ticket Type   Validity   Cost
BIT (standard ticket):   100 minutes, includes 1 metro ride (€1.50)
Roma 24H: 24 hours unlimited travel, €7.00
Roma 48H: 48 hours unlimited travel   €12.50
Roma 72H: 72 hours unlimited travel, €18.00
CIS (Weekly):   7 days unlimited,   €24.00

Tickets can be bought from vending machines in stations (accepting coins and cards), Tabacchi shops (tobacconists), or on mobile via the myCicero or TabNet apps.

Always validate your ticket at the start of your journey. Failure to do so can result in a hefty fine, even if you have a valid pass.

Hours of Operation
Daily: 5:30 AM – 11:30 PM

Friday & Saturday: Extended until 1:30 AM

Trains come every 3–5 minutes during peak hours and 7–10 minutes during off-peak

Warning: There is no 24-hour metro service in Rome. If you're out late, you'll need to switch to night buses, taxis, or walking.

Using the Metro—Step-by-Step Guide for First-Timers
Buy your ticket or pass from a station vending machine (choose English language option)

Validate it at the electronic turnstile or ticket machine

Follow signs for your line and direction (check end-of-line name)

Wait behind the yellow line on the platform

When the train arrives, allow people to exit before entering

Hold your bag in front of you—especially in crowded cars

Exit at your stop (doors open automatically or with a button, depending on train model)

Safety, Etiquette & Common Pitfalls
Pickpocketing
Most common at Termini, Spagna, Barberini, and Colosseo

Avoid distractions like music or phones

Keep all valuables in zipped bags worn in front

Never carry passports or large amounts of cash in your back pocket

Metro Cleanliness & Comfort
Line A is generally the cleanest

Line B can be older and louder

Trains are not air-conditioned except on the newest models

Accessibility
Many stations have elevators and escalators, but breakdowns are common

Not every station is accessible for wheelchairs or strollers—check before travel

Insider Tips
Want a quick view of the Colosseum? Sit on the left side of the train coming from Termini toward Colosseo.

Avoid Termini at night if you're alone—it's functional but not pleasant.

If you're staying near a metro station, book accommodation near Line A or B—it will make your entire stay more efficient.

Don't rely on the metro to reach Trastevere, Campo de' Fiori, or Piazza Navona—these areas require walking or buses.

Final Thought
Use the Metro When:

You're traveling between major landmarks (Colosseum ↔ Vatican ↔ Spanish Steps)

You're commuting from a hotel to Termini station or an airport bus

You're short on time and long on distance

You're traveling early morning or midday, not during rush hour

Avoid the Metro When:

It's rush hour, and you're not comfortable with crowds

You want to explore romantic alleyways or historical neighborhoods

You're traveling late at night, and safety is a concern

Rome's Arteries
While the metro system forms the skeleton of Rome's public transit, the buses and trams are the arteries that extend to every corner of the city—from the narrow medieval

lanes of Trastevere to the sprawling outer neighborhoods of Monteverde, EUR, and beyond.

Used by millions of Romans every day, the bus and tram network is both extensive and indispensable. But it's also notoriously complex, frequently delayed, and occasionally chaotic for first-time users. In this section, we'll break down how the system works, which routes are most useful for tourists, how to avoid frustration, and when buses or trams are the best (or worst) option.

Understanding the Bus System
Rome's bus system includes hundreds of lines, operated by ATAC, the same company that runs the metro. There are four major categories of bus routes:

1. Urban Lines (U)
Standard buses, numbered (e.g., 40, 64, 87, 492)

Run throughout the day (generally 5:30 AM to midnight)

Serve both locals and tourists

2. Express Lines (E)
Fewer stops, faster service (e.g., 40 Express)

Typically run along major roads, ideal for commuters and cross-city trips

3. Night Buses (N)
Operate after midnight until around 5:30 AM

Replaced metro and most day bus routes during nighttime hours

Numbers begin with "n" (e.g., n5, n15)

4. Peripheral Lines (P)
Reach areas outside Rome's central belt

Rarely used by tourists unless staying in far-flung hotels

How to Use a Bus in Rome

Plan Your Route

Use apps like

Moovit (most reliable for Rome)

Google Maps (often underestimates wait times)

ATAC Roma app (official, but glitchy)

Buy Your Ticket

Same tickets as metro (BIT, Roma Pass, etc.)

Buy from Tabacchi shops, vending machines at metro stations, or authorized newsstands

You cannot buy tickets onboard (unless using mobile app with QR code)

Wait at the Right Stop

Stops are marked with signposts listing all bus numbers and schedules

Each stop includes a vertical list of stops for each route

Stops can be shared by multiple bus lines

Board and Validate

Enter through front or middle doors

Validate ticket in the yellow machine onboard

If using a digital pass (Roma Pass), you may scan or show to transit authority upon inspection

Stay Aware

Stops are not announced audibly on most buses—follow your location using GPS or watch the screen

Press "Stop" button before your destination

Exit

Rear doors open when the bus stops; press door button if needed

Be mindful of sudden halts

The Most Useful Bus Routes for Visitors
While the full network is vast, a few lines are especially useful for tourists:

Bus 40 Express
Termini → Vatican (Piazza Pia)

Stops: Termini, Piazza Venezia, Largo Argentina, Ponte Vittorio

Fast, but often crowded—watch for pickpockets

Bus 64
Also Termini → Vatican

Notorious for pickpockets

Slightly slower and stops more often than 40 Express

Good route for Campo de' Fiori, Piazza Navona, and Corso Vittorio Emanuele II

Bus 81
Colosseum → Vatican via Circo Massimo, Piazza Venezia, Piazza Navona

Covers many major tourist sites in one ride

Bus 492
Useful for Piazza Barberini, Trevi Fountain, and Via del Tritone

Bus 87
Colosseum → Piazza Cavour (near Vatican)

Good for historical sightseeing route

Rome's Trams—Elegant but Limited

Rome's tram system is the lesser-known cousin of the bus and metro systems—quieter, cleaner, and older in feel. Trams are an efficient and scenic way to get around certain areas of the city, but they don't reach most tourist neighborhoods.

Popular Tram Lines for Visitors:
Line 8:

Trastevere → Piazza Venezia

Modern tram with high frequency

Excellent for getting to and from Trastevere quickly

Line 3:

From Villa Borghese area to Trastevere, passing the Colosseum

Great for combining park exploration with ancient sites

Line 19:

Connects Prati/Vatican area to Villa Borghese and further northeast

Longest line, scenic but not fast

Tram Pros:

Cleaner and more reliable than buses

Less crowded than the metro

Unique way to experience Rome's street life

Great for photographers or relaxed travelers

Tram Cons:

Coverage is limited (many popular tourist areas lack tram stops)

Can be slow during peak traffic hours

Service interruptions and maintenance not uncommon

Common Problems and How to Overcome Them

Delays: Rome's traffic is notoriously unpredictable; add buffer time if taking a bus to a reservation or train station.

Overcrowding: Avoid buses at rush hour or major tourist hours (11 AM–2 PM).

Strikes: Rome has regular transport strikes (sciopero)—check online or ask at your hotel.

Confusing stops: Bus stop names are often abbreviated—cross-reference with maps.

Travel Tip:

For high-stress transfers (e.g., to the airport or for a timed tour), do not rely solely on buses unless you know the route well. In those cases, metros or taxis are safer options.

Are Buses and Trams Right for You?

Best for:

Travelers staying in neighborhoods not directly served by the metro

Photographers, slow travelers, and cultural explorers

Getting to Campo de' Fiori, Trastevere, Piazza Venezia, and Jewish Ghetto

Not ideal for:

Those with strict schedules or tight appointments

Travelers with heavy luggage

People nervous about navigation or delays

Navigating the Network—Real Tools That Help

Moovit App: Most accurate and user-friendly, includes live wait times

Citymapper: Great for route planning and walking integration

Google Maps: Use cautiously—travel times often optimistic

ATAC Site: Official but clunky; real-time data often delayed

Download route maps and save them offline for moments when the signal is poor.

Taxis and Ride-Hailing Apps—Rome's Mixed Bag
Rome is a city where taxis are everywhere—and nowhere at once. You might find a dozen waiting at Termini Station but be stranded in Trastevere after dinner with none in sight. Add to that a mix of ride-hailing options, regulatory quirks, and rampant tourist overcharging, and you have a system that's both indispensable and infuriating.

This section unpacks how taxis work in Rome, how to book safely, what to expect in terms of pricing and etiquette, how to use apps like Uber, Free Now, and It Taxi, and how to avoid common scams.

Official Taxis—What to Look For
In Rome, legitimate taxis are

White

Have a "TAXI" sign on top

Display the city of Rome's municipal crest and license number on the side

Have a meter inside (on the dashboard)

Always ensure you're entering an official vehicle—never accept rides from unauthorized drivers or random individuals offering "taxi" services outside tourist sites or airports.

Finding a Taxi
Taxis in Rome do not stop when hailed like in New York or London—instead, you should:

Walk to a taxi stand (stazione taxi)—located near major squares, train stations, and tourist hubs

Call a taxi dispatch service (e.g., Radiotaxi at +39 06 3570)

Use a ride-hailing app (details in section 2.5.6)

Taxi stands are common at:

Termini Station

Piazza Venezia

Largo Argentina

Piazza di Spagna

Via Veneto

Campo de' Fiori

Vatican City (Via della Conciliazione)

If you see a free taxi and the light on top is on, you can try to flag it down, but drivers are not obligated to stop unless you're at a designated stand.

How Fares Work
Taxis in Rome use meters, and pricing is governed by municipal law. However, the system can still be confusing.

Standard Rates (Weekdays, 6:00 AM – 10:00 PM):
Base fare: €3.00

Per kilometer: €1.10 (up to 3 km), then drops to €0.90/km

Per hour (waiting/traffic): approx. €28.00

Night surcharge (10:00 PM – 6:00 AM): +€3.50

Sunday/Holiday surcharge: +€1.50

Flat Rates (to/from airports):
Fiumicino Airport (FCO) ↔ City center: €50 (fixed, includes luggage & up to 4 passengers)

Ciampino Airport ↔ City center: €31

Covers all addresses within the Aurelian Walls (central Rome)

Note: Fares may increase outside the city limits, with an added per-kilometer cost after leaving Rome proper.

Tipping, Luggage, and Etiquette
Tipping is not obligatory, but rounding up to the nearest euro or adding €1–€2 is appreciated.

Luggage fees are often waived, but some drivers may add €1 per bag—technically legal, though not common.

Shared rides are possible if everyone agrees beforehand.

It's polite to greet your driver with a "Buongiorno" or "Buonasera" and confirm your destination before departure.

Avoiding Taxi Scams
Unfortunately, some taxi drivers target tourists with tricks to overcharge. Here's how to avoid the most common scams:

1. "Broken meter" trick
Solution: Immediately exit the cab if no meter is running, or refuse the ride

2. Taking longer routes
Solution: Use Google Maps during your ride and call out detours

3. Charging extra for luggage, passengers, or holidays
Solution: Know the flat airport rates and legal surcharges

4. Quoting "flat fee" inside the city
Solution: All city rides must use the meter, unless you're going to/from the airport

Travel Tip: If you feel scammed or overcharged, take a picture of the taxi license number and report it to Municipal Police (Polizia Municipale) Or call 060606, the City of Rome helpline (English available)

Ride-Hailing Apps in Rome—A Legal Gray Zone
Italy has tight regulations on ride-hailing services, and Rome enforces them strictly. While Uber exists, it operates in a limited form.

Uber
Only operates Uber Black, Uber Lux, and Uber Van in Rome

No UberX—meaning no budget rides

Prices are often higher than taxis, but cars are luxurious (Mercedes, BMW, etc.)

Drivers are licensed NCC (chauffeurs)—not regular taxi drivers

Free Now
Popular in Europe, works well in Rome

Connects to licensed taxis, not freelancers

You can prebook or pay through the app

Prices match metered fares

It Taxi
Italian-based app connected to Rome's taxi network

Works like Free Now—gives you access to licensed drivers

Can call, track, and pay in-app

myTaxi (Now Free Now)
Previously available—has merged with Free Now in most areas

When Should You Take a Taxi or Ride-Share?
Recommended:

To/from airports or train stations, especially with luggage

Late at night when buses and metros stop running

If you're lost or far from public transport routes

When traveling with small children, elderly, or individuals with mobility challenges

In poor weather

Avoid when:

Traveling short distances in areas with high traffic

During rush hours (8:00–10:00 AM, 5:00–7:30 PM)

On Fridays and Saturdays late night in Trastevere and Testaccio, availability becomes scarce and pricing may surge on apps

Taxi or Uber—Which Should You Choose?

Criteria	Official Taxi	Uber Black/Free Now
Availability	High in central areas	Medium
Cost	Lower (fixed pricing)	Higher (luxury tier)
Comfort	Moderate	High-end cars
Booking method	stand, phone, app	app only
Reliability	Variable	Consistent
Tourist protection	Mixed	Better with app records
English-speaking drivers	Rare	more likely

Pro Tip:
If you're nervous about hailing a taxi or dealing with cash, use Free Now—it offers the structure and convenience of an app while giving you access to official taxis.

Summary—The Do's and Don'ts

Do:

Use only licensed taxis or regulated apps

Confirm airport fares before boarding

Monitor the route using GPS

Know surcharges and legal rights

Don't:

Accept unlicensed rides

Ride without the meter running

Assume Uber works like in other countries

In side streets, expect to hail a cab; use an app or stand.

CHAPTER 3:

Neighborhoods, Hotels, and Unique Lodgings

Finding the perfect place to stay in Rome isn't just about picking a hotel—it's about choosing the right neighborhood experience. Do you want to be surrounded by history and cobblestones, or do you prefer leafy calm away from the tourist bustle? Are you dreaming of a view over the Colosseum or planning a romantic escape in Trastevere's lantern-lit alleys? This chapter will walk you through every type of accommodation in Rome—from 5-star palaces to charming guesthouses, boutique hotels, monastery stays, family apartments, and budget hostels—and help you match your travel goals to the city's varied districts.

Expect detailed insights into:

The best neighborhoods for different travelers (first-timers, families, honeymooners, solo travelers, etc.)

Comprehensive guides to luxury, mid-range, budget, and alternative accommodation

Booking tips, scams to avoid, and how to get the best value

Accessibility, amenities, seasonal pricing, and local secrets that make all the difference

Let's begin with the essential decision: Where in Rome should you stay?

Understanding Rome's Neighborhoods

Rome is a sprawling city of layers—both ancient and modern. Each rione (district) offers a different atmosphere, rhythm, and proximity to major attractions. In this section, we'll cover the most popular and practical areas to stay, including their strengths, weaknesses, vibe, and hidden perks.

Centro Storico (Historic Center)

Ideal for: First-time visitors, art lovers, history buffs

The Centro Storico, or "Historic Center," is Rome's living museum—a maze of cobblestoned streets, Renaissance churches, elegant fountains, and bustling piazzas.

Staying here means you're walking distance from the Pantheon, Piazza Navona, Campo de' Fiori, and Trevi Fountain. It's hard to beat the romantic charm or the sheer density of cultural icons.

Accommodation Style: Boutique hotels, historic guesthouses, high-end B&Bs

Pros: Unbeatable central location, rich atmosphere, excellent food

Cons: Expensive, can be noisy and crowded, fewer modern amenities

Insider Tip: Some palazzi-turned-guesthouses retain original 16th-century frescoes and balconies

Trastevere
Ideal for: Couples, foodies, nightlife seekers, bohemian travelers

Charming, artistic, and delightfully Roman, Trastevere is full of character. Narrow alleys, ivy-covered buildings, and buzzing trattorias define the neighborhood. It's across the Tiber River but still very central—and perfect for those wanting culture without the tourist swarm.

Accommodation Style: Airbnbs, boutique hotels, cozy B&Bs

Pros: Romantic and lively, excellent restaurants, close to the Vatican

Cons: Uneven streets (tough for luggage), limited metro access

Insider Tip: Ask for a room facing the inner courtyard to avoid night-time street noise

Monti
Ideal for: Hip travelers, young couples, solo adventurers

Once a working-class zone, Monti has transformed into a stylish, artsy enclave. Tucked between the Colosseum and Termini Station, this neighborhood blends ancient history with indie shops, wine bars, and artisan cafes.

Accommodation Style: Design hotels, budget hostels, chic apartments

Pros: Close to ancient Rome, great nightlife, edgy and fun

Cons: Prices rising fast, streets can be hilly

Insider Tip: Stay near Via dei Serpenti for a direct Colosseum view from your room

Vatican/Prati
Ideal for: Religious pilgrims, museum lovers, quiet luxury seekers

Just outside Vatican City, Prati is an upscale, elegant area with wide boulevards, Art Nouveau buildings, and excellent shopping. It's quieter and less touristy but still central—ideal for travelers who want peace with convenience.

Accommodation Style: Mid-range hotels, guesthouses, religious houses

Pros: Safe, clean, sophisticated, excellent transport links

Cons: Less nightlife, longer walks to central Rome

Insider Tip: Book near Via Cola di Rienzo for boutique shopping without crowds

Testaccio
Ideal for: Food lovers, culture seekers, repeat visitors

Testaccio is where real Romans live. It's a neighborhood with soul—home to old-school trattorias, a famous food market, and some of Rome's best nightlife. If you want to skip the tourist track and experience daily life, Testaccio is unbeatable.

Accommodation Style: Budget hotels, local apartments, niche B&Bs

Pros: Authentic Roman atmosphere, affordable dining, fewer crowds

Cons: Farther from major attractions

Insider Tip: The local hill is made from broken amphorae—a secret archaeological site under your feet

Termini & Esquilino
Ideal for: Budget travelers, quick stays, transportation hubs

Near Rome's central train station, this area is often overlooked—but it offers Rome's best deals. Great for travelers arriving late or leaving early, it's also incredibly diverse and full of ethnic restaurants and hidden gems.

Accommodation Style: Budget hotels, hostels, short-stay rooms

Pros: Affordable, well-connected, multicultural food scene

Cons: Can feel gritty or busy at night

Insider Tip: Avoid streets directly opposite Termini station—quieter options lie just two blocks out

Accommodation Types in Rome—From Royal Suites to Budget Beds
Rome's accommodation scene reflects the city itself: layered, historic, and full of personality. Whether you're dreaming of a 17th-century palazzo with golden chandeliers, a minimalist design hotel tucked in a bohemian street, or simply a clean, reliable place to rest your head after hours of walking through ruins and piazzas, Rome has it all.

Luxury Hotels

Rome's luxury hospitality often inhabits buildings that were once the residences of popes, princes, or Roman aristocrats. If you're seeking elegance, comfort, and pampering, you'll find five-star hotels with Renaissance courtyards, rooftop gardens overlooking the Pantheon, and Michelin-starred restaurants tucked beneath frescoed ceilings.

Notable Features:
Suites with marble bathrooms, antique furniture, and Roman skyline views

Impeccable concierge services (private Vatican tours, dinner reservations, vintage car rentals)

Rooftop bars, in-house spas, and haute cuisine

Central locations—often within steps of Piazza di Spagna or Via Veneto

Popular Options:

Hotel de Russie (near Piazza del Popolo)—luxurious yet modern, with a legendary garden courtyard

J.K. Place Roma (Campo Marzio)—boutique opulence, marble elegance, unmatched service

Hassler Roma (top of the Spanish Steps)—traditional glamour with city-wide views

Palazzo Manfredi—direct Colosseum views from your breakfast table

Who It's For:
Honeymooners

High-end travelers

Business executives seeking elegance

Guests wanting a quiet, indulgent escape in the city center

Insider Advice:
Book at least 4–6 months in advance during spring and fall

Ask for "panoramic views" or "historic suite"—many are hidden gems within the listings

Don't skip the hotel concierge: they can unlock doors tourists never see

Mid-Range Hotels

Rome's mid-range accommodations can be a delightful surprise. Many are housed in renovated 19th-century buildings with original flooring, tall shuttered windows, and balconies that open over classic streetscapes. Some have stunning interiors that rival luxury hotels—minus the Michelin stars and spa wings.

Typical Features:
Clean, comfortable rooms with tasteful decor

Air conditioning, free Wi-Fi, and daily housekeeping

Breakfast included (usually a light Italian-style buffet)

Friendly local staff

Great Examples:
Hotel Artemide (Via Nazionale)—excellent service, rooftop restaurant, great location

Albergo del Senato—steps from the Pantheon with classic Roman charm

Hotel Santa Maria (Trastevere)—cloister-style garden hotel in the heart of a bohemian neighborhood

Hotel Damaso—stylish, well-priced, and central to major landmarks

Ideal For:
Couples and solo travelers wanting a quality stay without luxury pricing

Families who want more reliable comfort near major landmarks

Travelers valuing good service and authentic ambiance

Booking Tips:
Look for offers with "free cancellation" to keep your options open

Try to book hotels with rooftop access or internal courtyards for a quieter stay

Budget Hotels & Hostels

Rome is doable on a budget, especially if you're flexible and plan in advance. Budget doesn't always mean barebones—many places offer excellent value and character. You'll find everything from cozy, family-run pensioni to backpacker hostels with modern facilities and community energy.

Features:
Basic but clean private rooms (often with shared or en-suite bathrooms)

Communal kitchens or lounge areas

Central or semi-central locations (often near Termini or Monti)

Free Wi-Fi and simple breakfast

Recommended Options:
The Beehive (Termini)—eco-conscious, stylish, laid-back hostel-hotel hybrid

Freedom Traveller Hostel—great for solo backpackers and short stays

Hotel Italia—reliable, clean, and close to Repubblica Metro

Generator Rome—hip, industrial-chic hostel with events and social energy

Best For:
Students

Digital nomads

Backpackers

Weekend trippers

Budget Tips:
Avoid peak months (May–June, Sept–Oct) or book well in advance

Look for hostels with lockers and hotels with in-room safes

Don't expect elevators in older buildings—check accessibility details

Guesthouses and B&Bs
Rome has a strong tradition of family-run guesthouses, where travelers are treated more like houseguests than hotel clients. These places are often set in historic apartments, and their owners take genuine pride in sharing local knowledge.

What to Expect:
Personalized service and home-cooked breakfasts

Unique rooms—no two are alike

Often excellent locations at great prices

Standouts:
Maison Giulia—elegant rooms near Campo de' Fiori, warm hosts

A View of Rome—friendly B&B with Vatican views

Nicolò III a San Pietro—small, modern, and steps from the Basilica

Ideal Travelers:
Those who want local insights and a homey atmosphere

Travelers wanting more character than chain hotels

Solo visitors who enjoy light conversation over breakfast

Religious Lodgings
Rome offers unique stays in convents, monasteries, and church-run guesthouses. While these are not luxury destinations, they offer safe, serene, often beautiful stays with a side of spiritual tranquility.

Features:
Modest but spotless rooms

Quiet hours enforced

Simple breakfast (often included)

Affordable pricing, excellent security

Where to Find Them:
Suore di Santa Elisabetta (Vatican area)

Casa di Santa Francesca Romana (Trastevere)

Istituto Maria Santissima Bambina (behind St. Peter's)

Who It's For:
Solo female travelers

Pilgrims and religious travelers

Those seeking peace, simplicity, and safety

Vacation Rentals and Airbnbs
From lofts in Monti to terraces in Trastevere, Rome's short-term rental scene is thriving. These options offer the chance to shop in local markets, cook your preferred meals, and enjoy the rhythm of Roman daily life.

Pros:
More space, especially for families

Great for longer stays or working travelers

Kitchens and washing machines add convenience

Cons:
No daily cleaning

Self-check-in can be confusing

Some areas are over-saturated, leading to rising local rents and regulatory crackdowns

Safety & Legality Tip:
Only book registered apartments with official licenses. Hosts must display their registration number—avoid listings that don't.

Booking Your Stay

Whether you're planning a short Roman holiday or a two-week immersion into the Eternal City, booking your accommodation is a critical part of the experience. In a city with thousands of lodging options—many of which may seem indistinguishable at first glance—smart booking decisions can make the difference between a magical, hassle-free stay and an underwhelming one.

In this section, we'll cover everything you need to know about booking accommodations in Rome, including how to time your reservations, avoid scams, leverage local options, and make sure you're getting the best value for your needs.

When to Book

Rome is a year-round destination, but not all seasons are created equal when it comes to accommodation availability and pricing.

High Season (April–June, mid-September–October)
These months are Rome's peak travel seasons due to the mild climate and major festivals. Hotel prices can double or triple, especially around Easter and long weekends.

Book at least 3–6 months in advance for popular areas or highly rated stays

Flexible cancellation is worth paying extra for—weather or events can shift plans

Shoulder Season (March, July, November)
Prices start to dip, crowds lessen, and deals emerge. This is the sweet spot for budget-conscious travelers who still want great weather (especially in March and November).

1–3 months in advance is usually sufficient

Watch for sudden price spikes tied to conferences or religious festivals

Low Season (January–February, mid-August)
Hotel prices can drop by 30–50% in winter or during Ferragosto (August 15th), when many Romans leave town.

Last-minute deals are more common, but quality varies

Expect some businesses to be closed in August, especially locally run B&Bs

How to Book
Major Booking Platforms:
Booking.com: The widest range, with verified guest reviews and generous cancellation policies.

Hotels.com: Good for repeat users due to their reward nights.

Expedia: Often offers packages with flights, which may lower total costs.

Airbnb/Vrbo: Ideal for longer stays, especially if you want to cook or need multiple bedrooms.

Local Booking Tips:
Contact hotels directly after finding them online—they may offer better rates or free upgrades for direct bookings.

Use **MonasteryStays.com** for religious accommodations.

Check **TripAdvisor** for recent traveler photos and up-to-date conditions.

Look for These When Booking:
Cancellation policies: Always review them carefully. Some "non-refundable" bookings have hidden exceptions.

City tax: Rome charges a per-night tourist tax, often not included in initial pricing (typically €4–€10 per person per night).

Luggage storage: Crucial if your arrival or departure doesn't match check-in/out times.

Booking Red Flags—What to Watch Out For
Rome's immense tourism industry has unfortunately attracted some scams and misleading listings. Being aware of common red flags can protect you.

Signs of Trouble:
No license number listed (especially on Airbnb): All short-term rentals in Rome must be registered.

Photos that look too perfect: Run a reverse Google image search to check for stock images.

Hidden fees: Look for "cleaning charges" or "deposit requirements" buried in the fine print.

Overly vague location: If an address isn't clearly stated, it might be far from the city center or poorly connected.

Protect Yourself:
Read at least five recent reviews, focusing on noise, cleanliness, and location accuracy.

Use only platforms with buyer protection (avoid paying via bank transfer or unknown links).

Save all confirmation emails, receipts, and contact numbers offline.

Seasonality, Events, and Pricing Trends
Rome hosts dozens of global events that can influence hotel rates and availability. Even small local celebrations can affect entire districts. Knowing the annual rhythm of Rome helps in picking dates that match your budget and style.

Expensive Times to Avoid (unless attending):
Easter Week: Massive religious tourism, especially near the Vatican

June 2: Republic Day—parades and closures

Christmas & New Year: Special decorations and events, but higher prices

Hidden Gems for Booking:
Early December: Festive lights but fewer tourists

Mid-February: Off-season charm, low hotel prices, romantic for Valentine's Day

Mid-November: Quiet streets, mild weather, great restaurant access

Weekly Trends:
Weekdays (Mon–Thurs) are often cheaper than weekends in popular zones

Sundays are ideal for scoring deals in business-focused areas (like EUR)

Choosing the Right Stay for Your Length of Visit
How long you stay in Rome affects where you should stay:

1–3 Nights (Short City Break):
Stay in Centro Storico, Monti, or near Termini for walking convenience

Prioritize location and fast check-in over luxury or kitchen space

4–7 Nights (Full Rome Experience):
Mix location with ambiance—Trastevere, Prati, or Monti

Consider a B&B or apartment for a homier feel

8+ Nights (Slow Travel or Remote Work):

Airbnb or vacation rentals in local neighborhoods like Testaccio or San Giovanni

Look for monthly rates, amenities like washing machines, and quiet surroundings

Accessibility, Elevators, and Other Practical Details
Rome's architecture is beautiful but often not accessibility-friendly. Know what to expect—especially if traveling with elders, mobility needs, or heavy luggage.

Many buildings lack elevators, especially in Trastevere and Centro Storico

Cobblestone streets can be difficult with strollers or suitcases

Always check for air conditioning—not all old buildings have it

24-hour reception is not standard—plan late arrivals carefully

Local Insights
Staying in Rome is more than a logistical detail—it's a cultural immersion. The experience you have each morning and evening, in the spaces where you rest, interact, and reflect on your day, deeply shapes your relationship with the city. This section goes beyond room sizes and check-in times to uncover how to live like a Roman—whether you're in a luxury hotel, a modest guesthouse, or a vacation apartment. Here, the local rhythms, customs, and everyday interactions become part of your Roman story.

Breakfast in Rome
Unlike the sprawling breakfast spreads found in American or northern European hotels, Roman mornings are about simplicity and ritual. Expect something light, intentional, and deeply satisfying.

What to Expect:
Cappuccino and Cornetto (Italian croissant)—the classic pairing

Sweet options dominate: jam tarts, biscuits, yogurt, Nutella packets

Rarely any hot savory options like eggs or bacon (unless in a luxury hotel)

In small B&Bs, breakfast may be served in-room or as a voucher for a nearby bar

Pro Tip:

If your accommodation offers a voucher to a local café, embrace it. This puts you into the Roman morning rhythm—standing at the bar, exchanging pleasantries with locals, and sipping espresso with intention.

The Role of the Concierge and the Host
Whether you're in a five-star suite or a family-run pensione, your host is often your secret key to the city. Romans love to help guests—they are proud of their city and eager to share its best (and often secret) features.

How to Use Their Knowledge:
Ask for their favorite restaurant, not just "a good restaurant."

Get advice on best times to visit sights—locals know the flow of the day

Request insight on transport shortcuts or walking routes

Trust their instincts about tourist traps to avoid

In an Airbnb or rental, hosts often leave guides, maps, or personalized notes. These small touches—often absent from chain hotels—enrich your stay immensely.

Neighborhood Nuances
Rome is a city of micro-neighborhoods, each with its own atmosphere, dialect, and personality. Staying in one over another can drastically change the tone of your trip.

Examples:
Monti: Creative energy, artisan boutiques, hip cafes. Ideal for young professionals or solo travelers.

Trastevere: Bohemian and romantic, full of vines, candles, and local osterie. Best for evening strolls and late-night gelato.

Prati: Polished, elegant, and quieter. A favorite of families and return visitors. Close to the Vatican.

Testaccio: Gritty charm and real Roman soul. Loved by food lovers and locals. Great for longer stays.

Centro Storico: Busy, beautiful, and iconic—everything is steps away. But nights can be noisy, and restaurants touristy.

Advice:
Choose based on your pace. Want to be out till midnight? Trastevere. Prefer quiet mornings? Prati.

Don't judge a place by Google Street View—Rome's magic is often inside the buildings.

Living Among Locals—Markets, Bars, and Grocers
If you're staying in an apartment or B&B, you'll likely find yourself shopping, sipping, and strolling alongside Romans—and that's a gift.

Embrace These Local Spots:
Mercato di Testaccio: A local market where real Romans buy cheese, bread, produce, and wine.

Forno (bakery): Grab fresh focaccia or pizza al taglio for an impromptu lunch at home.

Bar (café): Morning espresso becomes part of your identity in the neighborhood.

Tabaccheria: Not just for cigarettes—this is where you buy bus tickets, stamps, and advice.

Etiquette Tips:
Say "Buongiorno" when you enter shops or cafes—it's expected and appreciated.

Don't rush. Small talk is part of the purchase.

Keep cash handy—some places still don't take cards.

Respecting the Roman Way of Life
Rome is welcoming but also traditional. Locals appreciate travelers who show cultural sensitivity, especially in shared or residential spaces.

Do:
Observe quiet hours (especially 2–4 p.m. and after 10 p.m.)

Sort your trash if your rental has recycling bins—it's mandatory in many areas

Use indoor voices in courtyards or stairwells

Greet your host or building porter with a nod or smile

Don't:
Assume staff will speak English fluently—basic Italian phrases go a long way

Treat apartment rentals like hotel suites—you're living in someone's neighborhood

Leave windows open with AC running—utility costs are high, and waste is frowned upon

Unexpected Perks of Staying Local
Travelers often report that their most memorable moments in Rome didn't come from tours or landmarks—they came from the quiet in-between spaces of daily life.

The elderly neighbor who smiled as you struggled with your door key

The barista who remembered your order by day three

The view from your rented apartment, just as church bells begin to toll

The conversation with your host that turned into a restaurant recommendation, then a magical evening

These are the moments you can't book online but which define what it truly means to stay in Rome.

Building a Daily Routine in Rome
Part of the joy of longer stays is creating your own rhythm. Don't feel compelled to fill every day with monuments and museums. Rome reveals itself slowly to those who dwell rather than dash.

Suggested Flow:
Morning: Walk to your favorite café for coffee, then take a quiet early visit to a museum or park

Midday: Return home for a nap or light meal from the market

Afternoon: Visit a local site or enjoy a walk through a lesser-known neighborhood

Evening: Watch the light change from your balcony or rooftop, then wander to dinner

CHAPTER 4:

Top Attractions in Rome

Rome is often described as a living museum, and nowhere is that truer than in the vast array of historical, architectural, artistic, and spiritual attractions that dot the city. From towering relics of the ancient Roman Empire to hidden chapels filled with Caravaggios, every corner offers a portal into another world.

The Colosseum—Empire, Blood, and Spectacle

The Colosseum as a Symbol

Few structures in the world hold the symbolic weight of the Colosseum. Known originally as the Flavian Amphitheatre, this vast arena stands as a staggering reminder of the power, spectacle, and contradictions of ancient Rome.

Standing in its shadow, one cannot help but reflect on its paradoxes: a monument to civilization and architecture—but also to violence and imperial dominance. Constructed in AD 72–80 under Emperors Vespasian and Titus, the Colosseum could seat over 50,000 spectators, who gathered to witness gladiator battles, animal hunts, and elaborate public spectacles.

Architecture—Engineering Brilliance

The Colosseum's engineering was—and still is—astonishing. This elliptical amphitheater measures 189 meters long, 156 meters wide, and 50 meters tall. It was built using travertine limestone, tuff (volcanic rock), and concrete, held together by iron clamps and careful balancing rather than mortar.

It featured

Velarium: a massive retractable canvas awning that shielded spectators from the sun.

Hypogeum: a two-level underground system of tunnels, lifts, and cages for animals and gladiators—the backstage of ancient Rome's most dramatic shows.

Seating tiers: strictly divided by class—senators in front, women and slaves at the top.

Today, as you walk among the ruins, you can still sense the incredible logistics that powered these shows—the pulleys, trapdoors, the roar of the crowd, and the scent of sand and blood.

Gladiators, Games, and Public Politics
While the spectacle of gladiators looms large in popular culture, these games were not just entertainment. They were tools of political propaganda, used to gain favor with the public and demonstrate imperial power.

Gladiators were slaves, prisoners of war, or volunteers (auctorati) seeking fame or fortune.

Venationes (wild animal hunts) brought exotic beasts from across the empire—lions, leopards, and elephants—and often ended in bloodshed.

Mock naval battles were staged in early years when the arena could be flooded.

Despite the brutality, these games reflected the social order of Rome. They entertained, yes, but also reinforced hierarchy, control, and ideology. Emperors attended to be seen, and their presence was a spectacle of its own.

The Colosseum Through the Ages
Over the centuries, the Colosseum evolved:

After the fall of Rome, it was used as housing, a fortress, and even a quarry for building materials.

In the Middle Ages, earthquakes and neglect damaged the structure.

By the 18th century, it became a site of Christian pilgrimage—believed to be a place of martyrdom.

Today, it's both a global icon and a UNESCO World Heritage Site, visited by over 7 million people a year. Conservation efforts continue, with new walkways and upper tiers opening to the public recently.

Visiting the Colosseum—What You Need to Know
Opening Hours:
Open daily (except Dec 25 & Jan 1)

Hours vary by season: usually from 9:00 a.m. to 5:00–7:00 p.m.

Tickets:
A standard ticket includes Colosseum, Roman Forum, and Palatine Hill

Optional: Guided tours, Arena floor access, or Underground experience

Tips for Visiting:
Buy in advance. Tickets sell out—especially for the underground or night tours.

Go early or late in the day to avoid crowds and harsh light.

If possible, book a guided tour—understanding the context vastly enhances your visit.

Bring water and wear comfortable shoes—it's larger and rougher than it appears.

Nearby Gems:
Arch of Constantine (right beside the Colosseum)

Colle Oppio Park—great viewpoint

Domus Aurea—the buried golden palace of Nero (advanced booking needed)

Experiencing the Atmosphere
To truly feel the Colosseum, don't just photograph it. Sit in silence. Listen. Imagine.

You are standing inside one of humanity's greatest—and most complex—creations.

The Roman Forum
Entering the Soul of Ancient Rome
More than any other site in the city, the Roman Forum (Forum Romanum) holds the spiritual and political essence of ancient Rome. While the Colosseum was the theater of power, the Forum was its boardroom, its altar, its courthouse, its parade ground—and sometimes its battlefield. It was the heart of Roman public life for centuries.

What now appears as a sprawling field of fragmented columns, broken arches, and marble rubble was once the most important gathering place in the Western world. Here, Cicero spoke, Julius Caesar walked, and Augustus forged an empire.

To step into the Forum is to walk the same path as emperors, senators, generals, and revolutionaries—a sensory and intellectual plunge into the foundations of European civilization.

Origins and Evolution

The Forum began humbly—a swampy valley between the Capitoline and Palatine Hills. Early Romans drained it in the 7th century BC with the Cloaca Maxima, one of the world's earliest sewage systems.

Over the next thousand years, it expanded into the nucleus of legal, religious, economic, and political life.

Temples to Saturn, Vesta, Castor, and Pollux

Basilicas (public halls) for commerce and law

Rostra (speaking platforms) where rhetoric shaped nations

Triumphal arches, monuments, and altars that made the abstract ideas of power and piety visible

The Forum was constantly changing—reflecting the turbulent shifts of Rome itself: republic to empire, paganism to Christianity, and power to decline.

What to See in the Forum

To truly appreciate the Forum, you must learn to read its ruins like pages in a history book. Each structure tells a story—of ambition, divinity, betrayal, or glory.

Here are some of the major highlights:

Temple of Saturn

Its eight towering Ionic columns dominate the western end of the Forum. Originally built in 497 BC, this temple housed the state treasury (aerarium) and honored Saturn, god of wealth and time. Fitting, as this was Rome's financial backbone.

Arch of Septimius Severus

One of Rome's best-preserved triumphal arches, this monument (203 AD) was erected to celebrate Emperor Septimius Severus' victories in Parthia (modern Iran/Iraq). Its marble friezes show detailed battle scenes—look closely to spot Roman soldiers crossing rivers on horseback.

Curia Julia (Senate House)
Unlike the other ruins, this building is intact. Rebuilt by Julius Caesar and later Augustus, it was the official meeting place of the Roman Senate. Inside, you can still see the marble flooring and sense the political gravity that once echoed through these walls.

Rostra
This was the platform from which leaders addressed the Roman people. It was decorated with the prows of captured enemy ships—hence the name "rostra." Mark Antony delivered Caesar's funeral oration here in 44 BC.

Temple of Vesta
A small circular temple, home to the eternal flame tended by the Vestal Virgins, priestesses sworn to chastity and responsible for the city's sacred fire. If the flame died, it was believed Rome itself would fall.

House of the Vestal Virgins
Adjacent to the temple, this tranquil courtyard was the residence of one of Rome's most revered and mysterious religious orders. Statues of past vestals line the garden path, each a symbol of purity and duty.

Basilica of Maxentius and Constantine
This massive ruin dominates the eastern side. It was once the largest building in the Forum, a marvel of Roman engineering with vaulted ceilings and marble columns. Its surviving arch gives a sense of its former grandeur.

Temple of Julius Caesar
Built on the spot where Caesar's body was cremated after his assassination. Romans still leave flowers and coins on his altar to this day—a poignant reminder of how personal history feels in this space.

Walking Through Time
Start from the Arch of Titus, at the eastern entrance near the Colosseum:

Enter via the Via Sacra (Sacred Way), the Forum's main road.

Move west toward the Basilica of Maxentius.

Stop at the Temple of Romulus, then swing through the House of the Vestals.

Pause by the Temple of Vesta and take in the Temple of Castor and Pollux.

Visit the Curia Julia, Rostra, and Arch of Septimius Severus.

Conclude at the Temple of Saturn, then climb toward the Capitoline Hill for a panoramic view.

Allow at least 2–3 hours, though you could easily spend half a day. Bring water, a hat, and a detailed map—signage is limited, and context is everything.

What the Forum Teaches Us
The Roman Forum is not just about architecture or ruins—it's about layers of meaning:

The continuity of law and public discourse

The rise and fall of ambition, of gods and men

The tension between order and chaos, politics and religion

In a single glance, you may see a temple from the Republic, a basilica from the Empire, and a church from the Renaissance, all coexisting—Rome compresses time like no other city.

Forum Tips & Nearby Sites
Best Time to Visit
Early morning for cool temperatures and fewer crowds

Late afternoon for golden light and shadows

Ticketing:
Access included in Colosseum combo ticket

Palatine Hill (next section) is connected—no need to exit

What to Bring:
Download an audio guide or app

Printed maps or illustrated guides add depth

Avoid relying on signage alone

Nearby Gems:
Capitoline Museums—ancient sculptures, Renaissance palaces

Mamertine Prison—where tradition says Peter and Paul were imprisoned

Piazza Venezia—climb the Vittoriano for epic views

Palatine Hill

Palatine Hill is the most legendary of Rome's seven hills. It is here, according to ancient lore, that Romulus founded Rome in 753 BC after slaying his twin brother, Remus. More than myth, however, the Palatine became the epicenter of imperial authority, evolving into the exclusive domain of Rome's emperors.

In fact, the word "palace" itself derives from the Palatine (Latin: Palatium), a testament to the vast complexes of opulence that once crowned this historic elevation.

Today, the Palatine offers more than just ruins—it provides a rare, peaceful reprieve from the city, with shaded gardens, towering pines, sweeping vistas, and ruins that whisper stories of gods, emperors, and ambition.

The Myth of Rome's Birthplace
The tale begins in mythology, where Palatine Hill is said to be the location of the Lupercal Cave, where the she-wolf (lupa) nursed the infant twins Romulus and Remus. After a dispute over the city's founding, Romulus killed Remus and established Rome.

Whether legend or reality, archaeological discoveries—including Iron Age huts from the 8th century BC—support the claim that this area was among the earliest inhabited parts of Rome.

A visit here is not just a historical walk but an immersion in the origin story of one of the greatest civilizations the world has known.

Imperial Palaces
As Rome transitioned from republic to empire, Palatine Hill transformed into the most exclusive real estate in the known world. Emperors from Augustus to Domitian built massive palace complexes that served both as homes and instruments of political display.

Some of the highlights include

The House of Augustus (Domus Augusti)
Simple by imperial standards, Augustus' residence reflects his public image as a modest leader. Inside, remarkably preserved frescoes, mosaics, and painted mythological scenes showcase early Roman interior art. Despite its modest scale, its symbolism was powerful: Augustus aligned himself with Rome's origins and divine favor.

The House of Livia
Believed to be the home of Livia Drusilla, wife of Augustus. It contains some of the most vibrant frescoes in Rome—scenes of gardens, birds, and fountains that create a tranquil illusion of nature. The artistry reveals the fusion of domestic intimacy and imperial propaganda.

Domus Tiberiana
Initiated by Tiberius, this palace extended toward the Forum and was one of the first to fully dominate the Palatine. Though mostly in ruins, its subterranean arches and staircases hint at the scale of construction and the evolving nature of palace design.

Domus Flavia and Domus Augustana (built by Domitian)
Domitian expanded the imperial complex into a vast architectural masterpiece:

Domus Flavia: The public wing—for audiences, receptions, and official ceremonies.

Domus Augustana: The private wing—with personal chambers, gardens, and a stadium-shaped peristyle for elite entertainment.

The ruins today evoke grandeur: colossal brick walls, fountains, exedra (semicircular niches), and the remains of thermal baths. Domitian's palace essentially covered the entire Palatine—a city within the city.

Farnese Gardens and Renaissance Additions

In the 16th century, Cardinal Alessandro Farnese built the first botanical gardens in Europe atop the ancient ruins, introducing

Terraced landscaping

Fountains and grottoes

Shady paths among citrus and laurel

The Farnese Gardens (Giardini Farnesiani) became a Renaissance marvel, blending classical ruins with Renaissance ideals of order and beauty. While overgrown in places today, they remain a peaceful oasis, offering hidden viewpoints over the Forum and Circus Maximus.

Must-See Highlights on Palatine Hill
Here are some of the key stops during your visit:

1. Palatine Museum
A compact but fascinating museum displaying artifacts unearthed on the hill—including statues, frescoes, pottery, and reliefs—some dating back to Rome's earliest days. It helps visualize what once stood above ground.

2. Cryptoporticus
A mysterious, vaulted underground corridor with frescoed walls, likely used as a secret passage or covered walkway between imperial residences. Cool and quiet, it evokes the sense of an ancient imperial whisper.

3. Stadium of Domitian
It is not an arena, as previously believed, but rather a private sunken garden or hippodrome reserved for the emperor's use. The rectangular shape and columned sides suggest it may have hosted private games or rituals. It's a poetic ruin—a symbol of power now overtaken by grass and birdsong.

4. Viewpoints
Don't miss the panoramic lookouts:

Over the Roman Forum—one of the best in the city

Over the Circus Maximus—imagine 250,000 Romans cheering chariot races

Toward the Aventine Hill—quieter, greener Rome in the distance

Practical Guide to Visiting Palatine Hill
Ticket Access
Entry is included with the Colosseum + Forum ticket.

Choose a Super ticket for access to the houses of Augustus and Livia and underground areas.

Best Times to Visit
Morning for shade and quiet (especially in summer)

Late afternoon for golden light over the ruins

What to Bring
Comfortable shoes—there are steep paths and uneven surfaces

Water—limited refill points

A guidebook or audio guide for historical context

Facilities
Small restrooms near the museum

Limited shade—bring a hat or umbrella

Accessibility
While some areas have ramps or paved walkways, much of the site is not fully accessible due to elevation, stairs, and uneven ground.

Why the Palatine Still Matters
Palatine Hill is more than a ruin. It's the narrative core of Rome—a palimpsest of myth, monarchy, and empire. From she-wolves to emperors, from rustic huts to sprawling palaces, it embodies the evolution of Rome from a legendary village to a global empire.

In its silence, it offers something rare in modern Rome: contemplation. To stand on Palatine Hill is to look both backward and inward, connecting with the very idea of Rome—eternal, layered, and always majestic.

The Pantheon

As you step into the Piazza della Rotonda, there's a moment of hushed astonishment that often overtakes even the most seasoned traveler. There, commanding the space with serene authority, stands the Pantheon—an ancient temple so perfectly preserved, so gracefully proportioned, that it seems eternal.

Originally constructed as a temple to all gods (pan-theos) and later transformed into a Christian church, the Pantheon is perhaps Rome's greatest architectural legacy, influencing buildings from the Florence Duomo to St. Peter's Basilica and even the U.S. Capitol.

Its massive dome, still the largest unreinforced concrete dome in the world, is an engineering enigma, a spiritual symbol, and a cosmic calendar—all in one. More than 2,000 years after it was built, the Pantheon continues to defy age, gravity, and imagination.

Historical Origins and Transformations
Agrippa's Vision (27 BC)
The original Pantheon was built by Marcus Agrippa, a general and close friend of Augustus. The inscription still visible on the facade reads:

"M·AGRIPPA·L·F·COS·TERTIVM·FECIT"
("Marcus Agrippa, son of Lucius, made this building when consul for the third time.")

But this first structure burned down.

Hadrian's Masterpiece (c. 118–125 AD)
The present building was commissioned by Emperor Hadrian, who admired Greek classicism and Roman innovation. In typical humility (or political calculation), Hadrian retained Agrippa's inscription. The Pantheon we admire today is Hadrian's reinvention—a space that fuses mathematics, cosmology, theology, and engineering into a single architectural experience.

Christian Church (609 AD–Present)
In the 7th century, the Byzantine emperor Phocas gifted the Pantheon to Pope Boniface IV, who converted it into Santa Maria ad Martyres. This transformation saved it from destruction, as pagan temples were often pillaged or dismantled in medieval times. Since then, the Pantheon has been in continuous use—a rare feat for any building, especially one over 1,800 years old.

Architectural Marvel
The Pantheon's genius lies not just in its size but in its harmony, innovation, and symbolism.

The Portico (Front Entrance)

16 Corinthian columns, each 39 feet tall, made of Egyptian granite, transported to Rome by sea and river.

The pediment once held a gilded bronze sculpture.

The vast entryway leads visitors from the chaotic square into a realm of calm and precision.

The Rotunda and Dome
Inside, the Pantheon's circular form measures 43.3 meters (142 feet) in diameter—equal to its height, forming a perfect sphere. This symmetry creates a sense of divine order and balance.

The oculus (Latin for "eye") at the dome's center is a 9-meter-wide hole open to the sky. It is the only source of natural light, creating a moving beam that sweeps across the interior like a celestial sundial.

The coffered ceiling reduces the weight of the dome without sacrificing strength and adds aesthetic depth.

The materials change by height—heavy basalt at the base, light pumice near the top—showcasing Roman engineering wisdom.

The dome's proportions and structure were not equaled for over 1,300 years. Brunelleschi studied it for Florence's cathedral; Michelangelo revered it while designing St. Peter's.

Floor and Interior
The floor is subtly convex at the center, allowing rain from the oculus to drain away.

The elegant pattern of colored marble—from Egypt, Tunisia, and Greece—reflects Rome's global reach.

Niches around the perimeter originally housed statues of gods, later replaced with Christian saints and martyrs.

The Pantheon as a Religious Space
The Pantheon's spiritual journey is complex—from pagan temple to Christian church to a monument to kings and artists.

As a pagan temple, it honored all gods, embodying the Roman virtue of religious inclusiveness and imperial power.

As a Christian church, it was rededicated to Mary and all martyrs, symbolizing the triumph of monotheism over classical polytheism.

It remains active today, hosting Masses, concerts, and the Feast of All Saints.

Yet its architecture continues to evoke a cosmic spirituality: the oculus represents the heavens, the dome the firmament, and the circle the perfection of the divine.

Tombs and Memorials Inside the Pantheon
The Pantheon is also a resting place for great Italians:

Raphael, the beloved Renaissance painter, was buried with an epitaph by Pietro Bembo: "Here lies Raphael, by whom Nature feared to be outdone while he lived, and when he died, feared she would die too."

King Victor Emmanuel II, Italy's first king, and Umberto I, his successor, along with Queen Margherita.

Several other artists and monarchs were interred or memorialized here, cementing the Pantheon's role as a national shrine.
Experiencing the Pantheon—What to Notice
To appreciate the Pantheon fully, stand in the center under the oculus and look up. You'll feel:

A powerful sense of cosmic connection

The play of light and shadow moving like a celestial clock

The silence that seems to amplify thought

Now walk slowly around the perimeter, taking in:

The way each niche balances the others—a lesson in harmony

The change in acoustics under the dome and toward the apse

The details in marble, metal, and stone—subtle, never ostentatious

On a rainy day, you'll witness water pouring through the oculus—a surreal spectacle.

On 21 April (Rome's birthday), the midday sun beams directly through the oculus onto the doorway—a cosmic celebration encoded in architecture.

Visiting the Pantheon
Admission
Entry is now ticketed (free for Rome residents and those under 18).

Book in advance to skip the queue, especially in summer.

Opening Hours
Usually open daily, except on major holidays.

Early mornings offer the best light and the fewest crowds.

Guided Tours
Highly recommended—many layers of history and symbolism aren't obvious.

Look for specialized architectural or art history tours.

Nearby Attractions
Piazza della Rotonda: Sit with a coffee or gelato and watch the light shift on the Pantheon's facade.

Church of San Luigi dei Francesi: just nearby, home to three Caravaggio masterpieces.

Piazza Navona, Campo de' Fiori, and Via del Corso are all a short stroll away.

Why the Pantheon Still Stands
The Pantheon's longevity is no accident. It reflects

Roman material genius: using concrete, pozzolana (volcanic ash), and sophisticated weight distribution

Architectural vision: a building not just for function but for awe

Symbolic unity: earth and sky, gods and humans, time and eternity

It was—and still is—an act of cosmic architecture: built not just to house the gods, but to mirror the universe itself.

Piazza Navona

Few places in Rome encapsulate the city's soul as vividly as Piazza Navona. Here, the rhythm of Roman life beats in full color: street musicians strum guitars, painters sketch portraits, children chase pigeons, and lovers share whispered secrets under Bernini's theatrical fountains.

Piazza Navona is an open-air masterpiece, rich with layers of history, art, architecture, and culture. Originally built upon the foundations of Domitian's Stadium, the square today reflects the grandeur of Baroque Rome, shaped by papal ambition, artistic rivalry, and public ritual.

Whether by day or night, Piazza Navona is a place of movement, conversation, performance, and passion—the very essence of Roman vitality.

From Roman Arena to Baroque Extravaganza
The Stadium of Domitian (1st Century AD)

The origins of Piazza Navona lie in the 1st century AD, when Emperor Domitian commissioned a stadium to host athletic competitions (agones), modeled after Greek games.

It could hold around 30,000 spectators.

The arena measured 276 meters long and 106 meters wide.

It was used for foot races, wrestling, and possibly gladiatorial contests.

The shape of the modern piazza still mirrors the outline of the ancient stadium, and beneath the northern end, visitors can descend into the Stadium of Domitian ruins, now an underground museum.

Transformation into a Baroque Square (17th Century)

Fast forward to the 1600s, when Pope Innocent X (Pamphilj family) decided to turn the square into a showcase of papal prestige. He commissioned the construction of

Palazzo Pamphilj, the family palace.

Sant'Agnese in Agone, a church built on the site of a martyrdom.

And, most famously, the Fountain of the Four Rivers, by Gian Lorenzo Bernini.

The piazza thus became a Baroque theater, combining politics, faith, and artistry in the most Roman way possible.

The Fountains—Water as Spectacle
Piazza Navona is home to three monumental fountains, each with its own character and story.

1. Fontana dei Quattro Fiumi (Fountain of the Four Rivers)
At the center stands Bernini's 1651 masterwork—a towering obelisk rising from a rocky base surrounded by allegorical river gods, representing the known continents and their great rivers:

The Nile (Africa)—his head is covered, symbolizing mystery.

The Ganges (Asia)—holds an oar, indicating navigability.

The Danube (Europe)—touching the papal coat of arms, symbolizing proximity to Rome.

The Río de la Plata (Americas)—seated on coins, referencing riches and colonial greed.

The base includes exotic animals, plants, and dynamic water movement. The entire piece is a celebration of papal power and a nod to Rome's global dominance under Christianity.

Bernini's design was controversial and revolutionary: he made solid stone appear light, dynamic, and natural—a living scene in motion. This fountain is not just sculpture; it is narrative and propaganda in marble.

2. Fontana del Moro (Southern End)
Originally designed by Giacomo della Porta in the 1570s, it features a basin with tritons and dolphins. Bernini later added the central figure—a muscular African man, or "Moor," wrestling with a dolphin.

It is playful, dramatic, and theatrical—showcasing the Baroque flair for exaggeration and action.

3. Fontana del Nettuno (Northern End)

Also begun by della Porta but completed much later in the 19th century, this fountain shows Neptune battling a sea monster, surrounded by graceful sea nymphs and cherubs.

It balances the symmetry of the square and continues the theme of mythological drama and marine power.

Sant'Agnese in Agone

Opposite Bernini's fountain rises the ornate Church of Sant'Agnese in Agone, begun by Francesco Borromini, Bernini's rival.

The church marks the site of St. Agnes's martyrdom, where, according to legend, the young girl was stripped naked and miraculously protected from shame before being executed for her Christian faith.

The church façade is a masterpiece of Baroque architecture, curving inward to embrace the piazza, with soaring twin bell towers framing the dome. Inside, the church is richly decorated with stuccoes, frescoes, and polychrome marble.

The architectural rivalry between Borromini and Bernini added an extra layer of drama: popular myth holds that the river god of the Nile covers his face to "avoid seeing" Borromini's church—though this was chronologically impossible. Still, the legend persists and feeds the piazza's lively lore.

Palazzo Pamphilj

Next to the church is Palazzo Pamphilj, the residence of Pope Innocent X and his powerful family.

Designed by Girolamo Rainaldi and Francesco Borromini.

It includes a splendid gallery frescoed by Pietro da Cortona, depicting the glory of the Pamphilj.

Today, it houses the Brazilian Embassy and is partially open for guided tours.

From the palace, the pope could observe events in the square below, turning the piazza into his personal stage.

Festivals, Traditions, and Life Through the Ages
Piazza Navona has long been a site of public celebration and spectacle.

Baroque Water Games (Laghetti)
In the 1600s and 1700s, the square was intentionally flooded in summer by plugging the fountain drains. The resulting shallow pools (laghetti) allowed carriages and people to splash around, cooling off in dramatic fashion.

Christmas Market
To this day, Piazza Navona hosts Rome's most famous Christmas market, complete with

Stalls selling candy, ornaments, and toys.

A carousel for children.

Live performers and seasonal music.

Traditional statues of La Befana, the Italian Christmas witch.

Artists and Performers
For centuries, the square has attracted painters, caricaturists, musicians, and street artists, adding a dynamic layer of energy to the space.

Experiencing Piazza Navona
A visit to Piazza Navona is not about checking boxes—it's about soaking in the atmosphere.

In the morning, enjoy a cappuccino at a quiet café and admire the light on the fountain statues.

Midday: Sit in the shade and people-watch as tourists mingle with locals.

Evening: return for the golden glow of sunset, or linger over dinner with the hum of violin and laughter in the air.

Night: Under spotlights and moonlight, the square feels theatrical—alive with echoes of Rome's layered history.

Don't rush. Sit. Breathe. Observe. This is Rome at its most romantic, sensual, and spectacular.

Practical Information
Getting There
A short walk from Campo de' Fiori, the Pantheon, or Piazza Venezia.

Nearest bus stops: Corso Rinascimento or Piazza Argentina.

Accessibility
Entirely pedestrian and flat, with benches and accessible paths.

Best Times to Visit
Early morning or late evening for photography and quiet ambiance.

Night for romance and magical light.

Dining
The piazza is ringed with restaurants—some overpriced, but a few hidden gems lie in nearby alleys. Ask locals or venture to Via del Governo Vecchio for more authentic cuisine.

In Piazza Navona, the past and present coexist in joyful tension. It is at once

An ancient Roman stadium

A Baroque opera set

A neighborhood living room

A tourist magnet

A sacred space

A place for espresso, memory, and love

This piazza doesn't just tell stories—it performs them, every hour of every day.

Campo de' Fiori

Just a short walk from the theatrical grandeur of Piazza Navona, Campo de' Fiori offers a sharper, earthier, and more unfiltered portrait of Rome. It is a place of contradictions:

A flower-filled square named "Field of Flowers," yet once the stage for public executions.

A hub of scholarly ideas and radical defiance, yet now pulsing with rowdy nightlife.

A historic market that still thrives, selling spices, vegetables, oils, and chatter.

Campo de' Fiori is not polished or ceremonial—it is gritty, lively, and unapologetically Roman. If Piazza Navona is an open-air opera, then Campo de' Fiori is a tavern with a poet in the corner and a revolution on the tip of its tongue.

The Origins

The name Campo de' Fiori literally means "field of flowers." In ancient times, this area lay outside the original city boundaries and remained undeveloped for centuries—a meadow of wildflowers near the Tiber.

Its transformation began during the Renaissance, when powerful Roman families and merchants invested in the neighborhood. The square became a commercial and cultural hub by the 15th century.

Streets nearby were named after professions: Via dei Baullari (trunk makers), Via dei Cappellari (hatters), and Via dei Giubbonari (tailors).

Inns, taverns, and stables opened for pilgrims and traders arriving at Porta Portese, the southern gate to the city.

Despite this growth, Campo retained its unrefined, working-class character, contrasting sharply with the aristocratic flair of adjacent piazzas.

The Shadow of Giordano Bruno

At the center of Campo de' Fiori stands a somber bronze statue of Giordano Bruno, philosopher, mathematician, and martyr of free thought.

Who was Bruno?

Born in 1548, Bruno was a Dominican friar turned cosmological radical.

He argued that the universe was infinite, that stars were suns with their own planets, and that God was present in all things—ideas that clashed violently with Church doctrine.

He was also a critic of institutional religion and questioned the authority of the papacy.

Trial and Execution
After years of wandering Europe, excommunicated and banned in multiple countries, Bruno was arrested by the Roman Inquisition and held for eight years.

On February 17, 1600, he was burned alive in Campo de' Fiori, defiant to the end.

His statue, erected in 1889 during the rise of Italian nationalism and secularism, faces the Vatican defiantly, reminding passersby that Rome's beauty is not just sacred but scarred and contested.

Bruno is now a symbol of intellectual freedom, and his statue draws pilgrims of a different sort—philosophers, atheists, artists, and rebels.

4.6.4 The Morning Market: A Feast for the Senses
Every morning (except Sunday), Campo de' Fiori transforms into a vibrant outdoor market, carrying forward a tradition that spans centuries.

What You'll Find:
Seasonal produce: figs, artichokes, tomatoes, and truffles.

Local cheeses: pecorino romano, buffalo mozzarella.

Cured meats: prosciutto, guanciale, and salami al tartufo.

Breads: crusty ciabatta, fragrant focaccia, pane casareccio.

Spices and dried herbs: saffron, oregano, and peperoncino.

Limoncello, olive oils, balsamic vinegar, and artisan pastas.

Stall owners shout deals in the Romanesco dialect. Locals haggle over fennel. Tourists sample sun-dried tomatoes with a glass of wine. A bag of porcini mushrooms may come with a joke, a wink, and a family recipe.

It's food culture at its most raw and intimate, a chance to connect with Roman life beyond museums.

Campo by Night
As the sun sets and market stalls disappear, Campo de' Fiori shapeshifts once again—into a boisterous center of nightlife.

The square fills with students, travelers, locals, and expats. Beer bottles clink. Pizzerias overflow. Laughter and music spill out from pubs and enotecas. It's chaotic, sometimes rowdy, but never dull.

Notable Spots Include:
La Vineria—A cozy wine bar with an extensive local selection.

The Drunken Ship—Popular with American students, known for beer pong and shouting.

Forno Campo de' Fiori—famous for its pizza bianca and simple, delicious Roman street food.

Caffè Farnese—Tucked nearby, with a view of Palazzo Farnese.

While not to everyone's taste, Campo's night scene captures Rome's living pulse, especially among younger crowds and backpackers.

Streets of History
Campo is encircled by layers of narrative. Step into the surrounding alleys, and you'll find

1. Via dei Giubbonari
Once lined with tailors, now filled with boutiques and leather shops.

Home to Roscioli, one of Rome's most famous delicatessens and restaurants.

2. Palazzo Farnese
Overlooking the square is this majestic Renaissance palace, once home to the powerful Farnese family.

Now houses the French Embassy and is known for its Michelangelo-designed facade.

3. Via del Pellegrino
Narrow and medieval, once a pilgrim route. Today, a charming blend of antique stores and local trattorias.

4. Ghetto Ebraico (Jewish Ghetto)
A short walk away, with layers of complex history, unique cuisine, and emotional depth—more on this in Chapter 6.

Campo in Literature and Film
Campo de' Fiori has inspired generations of artists and writers.

Featured in works by Pier Paolo Pasolini, who found poetry in its contradictions.

The setting for countless films that explore Rome's romantic and rebellious spirit.

A favorite subject for painters capturing the movement, market stalls, and expressive Roman faces.

Practical Information
Market hours: Monday–Saturday, 7:00 AM to 2:00 PM.

Best time to visit: early morning for the market or early evening before nightlife peaks.

Safety: Generally safe, but watch for pickpockets in crowded areas at night.

Dining tips: Step away from the square for better food prices and quality.

Why Campo de' Fiori Matters
Campo de' Fiori is more than a piazza. It is a mirror of Roman identity:

Its intellectual courage in the statue of Bruno.

Its daily life and commerce in the market.

Its urban grit and rebellious heart are in its taverns and alleys.

Its palimpsest of joy and sorrow, still legible in the cobblestones.

Here, you don't just observe history—you feel it under your feet, smell it in the fennel sausage, hear it in the shouts of vendors, and drink it down with a glass of Cesanese red.

CHAPTER 5:

VATICAN CITY

Entering the Vatican: A Nation Inside a City
Few places in the world inspire such reverence and awe upon approach as Vatican City. Nestled on the western bank of the Tiber River and enveloped on all sides by the city of Rome, this tiny sovereign city-state measures just 0.49 square kilometers (109 acres). And yet, within this compressed footprint lies a cultural, spiritual, and political force that has shaped world events for two millennia.

Entering Vatican City feels like traveling back in time rather than into a different nation. The atmosphere changes palpably as you pass beneath the ancient Roman walls into a space where centuries of tradition, devotion, diplomacy, and artistry converge.

This is not only the spiritual headquarters of the Roman Catholic Church but also the residence of the Pope, the repository of Renaissance genius, the location of the world's most famous religious architecture, and one of the greatest art collections on Earth. Vatican City is a place of pilgrimage, not only for millions of Christians, but also for art lovers, historians, architects, political scientists, and spiritual seekers from every corner of the world.

The Vatican cannot be reduced to a single identity because it is simultaneously:

A living museum of divine inspiration and human creativity,

A spiritual capital for over a billion faithful,

A micro-nation with diplomatic clout,

A keeper of secrets and traditions stretching back to antiquity.

We will examine every aspect of the Vatican as this chapter progresses, from the splendorous St. Peter's Basilica and its secret tombs to the intricate Vatican Museums, the private gardens, the Apostolic Palace, and more.

But first, we need to go back in time, to the beginnings of Vatican Hill and the martyrdom that would sow the seeds of a widely accepted religion.

The Vatican's Origins

The Death of a Fisherman
Vatican Hill was a place of execution and exile before it was designated as holy ground. It was a gloomy suburb of ancient Rome, located just outside the city's holy perimeter, where slaves, criminals, and early Christians were put to death. Here, around 64 AD, under the tyrannical rule of Emperor Nero, Saint Peter, the apostle of Jesus and first bishop of Rome, was executed.

Early Christian tradition holds that Peter requested to be crucified upside down, feeling unworthy to die in the same manner as Christ. His body was hurriedly buried in a nearby necropolis, little more than a humble grave on an unremarkable slope. But in time, this would become the most sacred site in Christendom.

Over that grave now soars the dome of St. Peter's Basilica—a beacon of faith that has lasted nearly two thousand years.

From Martyrdom to Monument
Three centuries later, Christianity had spread like wildfire throughout the Roman Empire. With Emperor Constantine's Edict of Milan in 313 AD, Christianity was legalized. Soon after, Constantine initiated the construction of a vast basilica over Peter's grave—a monumental gesture of imperial endorsement.

This original Old St. Peter's Basilica would stand for over a thousand years. It was a place of pilgrimage for medieval Christians, a center of papal authority, and a burial site for countless popes. But by the 15th century, it had fallen into disrepair.

The Renaissance papacy, eager to showcase its glory and authority, made a bold decision: to raze the old basilica and build a new one—grander, holier, and more permanent. This decision would give birth to the Vatican we know today and trigger an artistic revolution.

The Rise of the Papal States and Temporal Power
From the 8th century to the 19th century, the Papal States stretched across much of central Italy. The pope wasn't just a spiritual leader—he was a king in all but name, commanding armies, levying taxes, and enacting laws. The Vatican was the nucleus of a theocratic realm, and its rulers often wielded as much power as emperors and kings.

While this power led to great achievements—the patronage of art, architecture, and scholarship—it also invited corruption, wars, and challenges to papal legitimacy. The tension between spiritual mission and political control has long haunted the Vatican's history.

The Loss of Territory and Birth of the Modern Vatican (Lateran Treaty)
By the 19th century, the unification of Italy posed an existential threat to the Pope's temporal rule. In 1870, Rome was captured by Italian forces, and the Papal States were dissolved. For nearly 60 years, popes considered themselves "prisoners in the Vatican," refusing to recognize the Italian state.

This standoff ended in 1929 with the signing of the Lateran Treaty between Pope Pius XI and Italian dictator Benito Mussolini. The treaty established Vatican City as an independent, sovereign nation, distinct from Italy, with the Pope as its head.

Thus, the modern Vatican was born—a religious state without a standing army, yet with embassies around the world; a kingdom of ideas, tradition, and belief, more powerful than many nations.

St. Peter's Basilica
When you stand in front of St. Peter's Basilica, you are standing not just before a church but before a symbol of over 2,000 years of spiritual devotion, political power, and artistic triumph. It is the largest basilica in the world, a center of worship for Catholics, a masterpiece of Renaissance and Baroque architecture, and the resting place of Saint Peter himself, the fisherman-turned-apostle who was the first bishop of Rome.

Built on sacred ground soaked with martyrs' blood, envisioned by multiple popes, and shaped by the hands of geniuses like Michelangelo, Bernini, Bramante, and Maderno, the basilica stands today not merely as a building, but as a statement of enduring faith and immense human creativity.

Let us now journey through this structure—from its historic foundations and awe-inspiring architecture to the treasures it holds and the spiritual rituals it continues to host each day.

The Foundations
Before the majestic dome ever pierced the Roman skyline, there stood the Old St. Peter's Basilica, built in the 4th century by Emperor Constantine. It was a long basilica with a wooden roof, mosaics, and a focus on the tomb of St. Peter beneath the main altar. For over a thousand years, it served as the spiritual center of the Church. But as centuries passed, the structure weakened and decayed.

By the late 1400s, the Renaissance papacy saw an opportunity: to rebuild the basilica entirely, turning it into a visual declaration of the Church's power and renewal. Pope

Julius II laid the foundation stone in 1506, and so began the most ambitious architectural project of the early modern era—one that would span 120 years, multiple papacies, and conflicting artistic visions.

The Architects of the Sacred
The new basilica's construction brought together a who's who of Renaissance and Baroque art:

Donato Bramante envisioned a bold Greek cross design crowned by a massive dome—a structure of divine proportions.

Raphael modified Bramante's designs but died young.

Antonio da Sangallo the Younger refined it further, expanding the choir and adding complexity.

Michelangelo, appointed at age 71, simplified the plan, introduced emotional clarity, and designed the breathtaking dome—a soaring symbol of heaven on earth.

After his death, Giacomo della Porta completed the dome in 1590.

Finally, Carlo Maderno extended the nave and created the grand Baroque façade, giving the basilica its familiar longitudinal layout.

What emerged was not just an architectural marvel but a synthesis of divine geometry, artistic genius, and theological ambition.

The Façade and the First Impressions
As you approach St. Peter's Basilica from St. Peter's Square, the facade looms above you like a celestial palace. Designed by Carlo Maderno and completed in 1612, it stretches 115 meters wide and 45 meters high.

At the top, a row of 13 colossal statues gaze out across the square:

Christ the Redeemer at the center,

Flanked by 11 apostles (excluding Judas),

And St. John the Baptist, the forerunner.

Below them, an inscription in Latin reads:

"IN HONOREM PRINCIPIS APOST PAVLVS V BVRGHESIVS ROMANVS PONT. MAX. AN MDCXII PONT. VII"
("In honor of the Prince of Apostles, Paul V Borghese, Supreme Pontiff, in the year 1612, the seventh of his pontificate.")

The immense central balcony, known as the Loggia of the Blessings, is where the Pope appears after election to deliver the "Urbi et Orbi" blessing—to the city and to the world.

Even before you step inside, the architecture speaks in the language of divine majesty and earthly authority.

Entering the Basilica
Passing through one of the five great bronze doors, visitors enter a narthex (entrance hall) nearly 100 meters long—itself larger than most churches in Europe. On the right is the Holy Door (Porta Sancta), which is opened only during Jubilee years, allowing pilgrims to pass through into a state of grace.

Then, you enter the nave—and time seems to halt.

The interior of St. Peter's can hold over 60,000 worshippers, but due to its flawless proportions, it doesn't feel overwhelmingly vast. The marble, gold, and frescoes invite the eyes upward, to the coffered ceiling and to the monumental dome high above.

Michelangelo's Dome
The dome is the architectural climax of the basilica—136 meters high from floor to cross. Inspired by Brunelleschi's dome in Florence, Michelangelo made this one taller, lighter, and more awe-inspiring.

On the interior ring, written in Latin in letters over two meters tall, is the famous inscription:

"TV ES PETRVS ET SVPER HANC PETRAM AEDIFICABO ECCLESIAM MEAM..."
"You are Peter, and upon this rock I will build my Church..." (Matthew 16:18)

The design leads the eye (and the soul) upward, a visual metaphor for the soul's ascent toward God.

Visitors can climb to the dome's summit via 551 steps (or partially by elevator), offering one of the most astonishing panoramic views of Rome and the Vatican Gardens.

Artistic Treasures Inside
St. Peter's Basilica is a museum of living faith. Among its countless masterpieces:

Michelangelo's Pietà (1499)— Near the entrance on the right, this tender sculpture of the Virgin cradling Christ's dead body remains one of the most emotionally powerful works in history. Michelangelo was just 24 when he created it.

The Baldachin (Baldacchino) – Designed by Gian Lorenzo Bernini, this massive bronze canopy (over 29 meters tall) marks the high altar, which sits directly above St. Peter's tomb.

The Confessio—a sunken chapel in front of the altar, where pilgrims descend a few steps to pray before the tomb of Saint Peter, illuminated by 99 golden lamps.

The Monument to Pope Alexander VII—Bernini's theatrical sculpture—depicts the Pope kneeling in prayer while Death emerges from below with an hourglass—a memento mori of papal mortality.

Numerous Papal Tombs—Over 90 popes are buried here, from early Christian martyrs to modern pontiffs like John Paul II.

The Role of the Basilica Today
Though many see it as a historical or artistic site, St. Peter's remains a working church, filled with daily Masses, major liturgical events, canonizations, papal audiences, and silent prayer.

It is a place where:

Popes are elected and buried.

Saints are honored.

Pilgrims receive sacraments,

Tourists discover faith through beauty.

The Dome, the Grottos, and Climbing to Heaven

At St. Peter's Basilica, the structure itself is a spiritual journey—not just across time, but across space. The building's design takes you upward toward the light, into the vast heavens where the soul might glimpse the divine, and downward into the earth, where apostles, saints, and popes rest in silent contemplation.

Nowhere is this experience more profound than in two key parts of the basilica: the Dome (Cupola) and the Grottos below. This vertical movement—skyward and subterranean—echoes a universal spiritual motif: ascension and descent, resurrection and humility, glory and death. This section invites you to experience the Vatican in full vertical dimension.

Climbing the Dome
Michelangelo's Dome, a marvel of Renaissance engineering, is the architectural and symbolic apex of St. Peter's. Rising to a height of 136.5 meters (448 feet) from the base to the top of the cross, it remains the tallest dome in the world and the most powerful symbol of the Catholic Church's universal reach.

To climb the dome is to walk a path not only of physical effort but also of spiritual reflection. The journey upward invites awe, discomfort, introspection, and reward—not unlike the path of faith itself.

The Entrance and First Steps
You begin at the right side of the basilica, where a modest sign points to "Cupola." From here, you can choose

Elevator to the terrace, followed by 320 steps to the top,

Or the full 551 steps on foot—a physically demanding climb.

Whichever you choose, the first section leads you to the base of the dome, just above the nave, where you can look down into the basilica and gaze up into the interior of the cupola. Here, you see close-ups of the mosaic inscriptions and figures of angels, saints, and symbols—all rendered in breathtaking detail.

The Narrow Spiral Ascent
As you continue upward, the walls begin to close in. The staircases become tighter, steeper, and more disorienting. In one part, you're climbing through a spiral corridor barely wide enough for one person. The curvature of the dome presses against you. Your hand runs along a rope for support.

The claustrophobia, the sweat, the darkness—all of it makes the moment you reach the light feel transcendent.

The Summit and the View
At last, you emerge into the open air—onto a small circular gallery that wraps around the lantern at the very top of the dome.

From here, the entire city of Rome is laid out below like a divine tapestry. You can see

St. Peter's Square and its Bernini colonnade, shaped like two open arms embracing the faithful.

The Tiber River winding through Rome,

The Pantheon, Castel Sant'Angelo, and the Janiculum Hill,

Even the Alban Hills in the far distance on a clear day.

It is one of the most stunning urban panoramas in the world—and also a place of spiritual reflection. Many pilgrims bring prayer cards or rosaries, offering silent devotion here, closer to the sky than they've ever been.

Descending to the Grottos
As dramatic as the ascent is, so too is the descent into the depths—for beneath the floor of St. Peter's lies an entirely different world.

The Vatican Grottos (Grotte Vaticane) are a vast subterranean complex beneath the main altar and the nave. Here, in silent shadows and marble corridors, centuries of popes, cardinals, monarchs, and martyrs lie buried.

Stepping into the Grottos is like walking through the bones of Catholic history.

Architecture of the Sacred Underground
The Grottos are located on the level of the original Constantinian basilica, giving you a rare glimpse into the basilica's ancient roots. They are dimly lit, hushed, and reverent. Pillars, arches, and tombs line narrow walkways. Every step resonates with centuries of worship and pilgrimage.

The ceiling is low. The air is cool. The sense of gravity—physical and spiritual—is overwhelming.

Notable Tombs and Shrines
Here in the Grottos are the tombs of over 90 popes, along with monarchs, cardinals, and saints. Among them:

Pope John Paul II—His white marble tomb is among the most visited, surrounded by fresh flowers and often silent prayer.

Pope Paul VI, Pope Benedict XV, and Pope Pius XII—great leaders of the 20th century, each buried with honor and simplicity.

Queen Christina of Sweden—a Lutheran monarch who abdicated her throne, converted to Catholicism, and moved to Rome. She lies here as a symbol of personal transformation.

Saint Peter's Sarcophagus—At the heart of the Grottos lies the Confessio, the shrine believed to house the remains of Saint Peter himself. It is enclosed behind glass and illuminated by flickering lights. Pilgrims often kneel or weep before it.

The Necropolis (Scavi)
Beneath even the Grottos, at a third, deeper level, lies the Vatican Necropolis—one of the most astonishing archaeological sites in the Christian world. This 1st-century Roman burial ground, discovered in the 1940s, is believed to contain the actual tomb of Saint Peter.

Access is strictly limited to 12 people per tour, with advanced reservations required. Visitors must be over 15 years old. The Scavi Tour, as it is called, is profound and unforgettable.

Walking Among the Dead of Ancient Rome
Inside, you walk through preserved streets of ancient mausoleums, marble inscriptions, and sarcophagi. The layout reflects a real Roman necropolis—a city of the dead.

At the tour's climax, you are brought before a shrine constructed in the 2nd century, known as the Trophy of Gaius. It is believed that this structure was built directly above the remains of Peter.

Nearby, archaeologists discovered bones belonging to a 60-70-year-old man, buried in a niche behind a red wall. Based on inscriptions, tradition, and historical evidence, many scholars and the Church believe these are the bones of Saint Peter.

No matter what you believe, the experience is moving, intimate, and heavy with meaning.

Symbolism of Ascent and Descent: A Spiritual Geography
The basilica's vertical design reflects a universal spiritual truth:

Upward: The journey to the cupola, filled with light, height, clarity, and vision, symbolizing the soul's journey toward God, glory, and eternity.

Downward: The descent into the grottos and necropolis, dark and solemn, reminding us of mortality, sacrifice, and the sacred ground where faith was born.

This architectural narrative is not accidental—it is theological. It invites pilgrims to climb toward divine hope while remaining rooted in human humility.

Practical Guide
Dome (Cupola) Access:

Entrance: Right side of Basilica exterior

Elevator + 320 steps: €10

Stairs only (551 steps): €8

Hours: 7:30 AM–6 PM (longer in summer)

Grottos:

Entry is free

Follow signs inside the basilica after the papal altar

Photography is discouraged

Scavi Tour (Necropolis):

Apply via the Vatican Excavations Office (email months in advance)

Limited access—only 250 visitors per day

Cost: ~€13–15

Duration: ~1 hour 15 minutes

Absolutely worth it

St. Peter's Square
Standing before the massive façade of St. Peter's Basilica, the soul is caught between awe and intimacy—between the magnitude of heaven and the embrace of the Church. This emotional choreography was not accidental. It was meticulously designed by Gian Lorenzo Bernini, the master of Baroque architecture and papal spectacle.

St. Peter's Square (Piazza San Pietro) is not just a plaza; it is an arena for faith, power, unity, and drama. With its sweeping colonnades, ancient obelisk, and spiritual geometry, the square orchestrates human emotion into a divine experience.

The Vision Behind the Square
When Pope Alexander VII commissioned Bernini to redesign the square in the mid-1600s, the idea was not just to create an entryway but to complete the transformation of St. Peter's into a universal center of Catholicism.

The square had to:

Welcome the faithful with open arms.

Magnify the basilica and reinforce its authority.

Guide pilgrims' movements through space and time.

Create a visual harmony between pagan Rome and Christian Rome.

Bernini's solution was bold: a theatrical ellipse, framed by four rows of Doric columns arranged in two sweeping semicircular colonnades. These colonnades form what he described as the "maternal arms of the Church," embracing the world and inviting it home.

Geometry and Spiritual Symbolism
The square is not square at all. It is an ellipse, measuring 320 meters long and 240 meters wide, with two focal points—the centers of each semicircle. Bernini positioned

two stone disks on the ground, marking those foci. Stand on one, and you'll see a perfect illusion: the rows of columns align, and the four layers appear as one single row—a miracle of perspective.

The Obelisk at the Center
At the center of the ellipse stands a 4,000-year-old Egyptian obelisk, brought to Rome by Emperor Caligula in AD 37 and placed here by Pope Sixtus V in 1586. It once stood in the Circus of Nero, where early Christians were martyred, possibly including Saint Peter himself.

Atop the obelisk is a bronze cross said to contain a relic of the True Cross of Christ. It's a perfect fusion of pagan and Christian symbolism: a monument that once represented empire and conquest now stands as a beacon of faith and redemption.

The Colonnades
Each colonnade consists of 284 Doric columns and 88 pilasters, arranged in four rows. These columns are massive—each over 13 meters (43 feet) high—yet the curvature makes them feel inviting rather than intimidating.

Statues of Saints
Above the colonnades stand 140 statues of saints, sculpted by Bernini's students between 1670 and 1703. Each saint is rendered with unique features, expressions, and postures. Together, they form a celestial congregation, bearing silent witness to the faithful below.

The design creates the sensation that the entire Church—past and present—is watching over the pilgrim.

The Basilica's Façade and Papal Balcony
Standing at the center of the square, you face the basilica's towering façade, built by Carlo Maderno in the early 1600s. It stretches 114 meters wide and is adorned with colossal Corinthian columns, relief sculptures, and statues of Christ, John the Baptist, and eleven apostles.

At the center is the famous Loggia of the Blessings, where the Pope appears for the Urbi et Orbi blessing on Easter and Christmas and where newly elected popes are introduced to the world.

Papal Events and Ceremonies
St. Peter's Square is the setting for:

Canonizations and beatifications,

Holy Week processions,

General Audiences with the Pope (Wednesdays),

Easter and Christmas Masses,

Jubilee Years, when special Holy Doors are opened.

Each event is designed to be visible, participatory, and emotionally resonant. The square becomes a stage where heaven and earth meet, watched by hundreds of thousands of pilgrims and broadcast to millions more.

The Fountains
Two ornate fountains stand on either side of the obelisk.

The northern fountain was designed by Carlo Maderno in 1613.

The southern fountain was added by Carlo Fontana in 1677, mirroring the first.

They symbolize life, purification, and baptism—the flowing grace of God washing over humanity. In Rome's hot climate, they also provide literal refreshment, offering both pilgrims and pigeons a cool reprieve.

Visiting the Square
Even outside liturgical events, St. Peter's Square is a spiritual playground, full of small details and deep symbolism. When visiting:

Stand on one of the perspective disks and see the colonnade illusion.

Look for the wind rose embedded in the pavement, marking the directions of the compass.

Notice the inscriptions near the obelisk, especially the dedication by Sixtus V.

Observe how the architecture pulls your gaze forward, preparing you for entry into the basilica.

Light, Space, and Theatricality
Bernini's background in theater heavily influenced his design. St. Peter's Square functions like a cosmic proscenium—a stage that manipulates light, space, and movement to elicit an emotional response.

Depending on the time of day and season, the light casts different shadows on the square. The obelisk becomes a sundial. The saints appear to move in the golden dusk. The sky above often forms a perfect blue dome that mirrors the cupola of the basilica behind it.

This is Baroque theology through architecture—emotionally powerful, dramatic, and infused with divine logic.

The Square at Night
At night, St. Peter's Square transforms. Gone are the crowds and camera flashes. The space is silent, lit by soft spotlights and glowing fountains. The façade of the basilica shimmers. The obelisk casts a long shadow across the paving stones.

To visit at night is to see the Vatican in meditation, stripped of performance, laid bare in solemn majesty.

It's the perfect place for silent prayer, journaling, or simply resting in the sacred silence of the Eternal City.

Practical Tips for Visiting St. Peter's Square
Open 24/7 – You can walk through the square at any hour.

Security checks apply only if entering the basilica.

Papal audiences take place most Wednesdays (book in advance through the Prefecture of the Papal Household).

Avoid peak heat in summer (midday), and arrive early for major events.

Final Thoughts
Few public spaces in the world hold the weight of 4,000 years of history. From pharaohs to caesars to popes, from martyrdom to miracles, St. Peter's Square is more than architecture—it is sacred geometry in motion. It draws pilgrims into its embrace, calms their hearts, prepares their souls, and lifts their eyes toward heaven.

It is the threshold between the world and the Word, between outer Rome and the spiritual heart of Christianity.

CHAPTER 6:

Vatican Museums and the Sistine Chapel

In a city already overflowing with ancient wonders, the Vatican Museums stand in a class of their own. They are not simply museums. They are a labyrinth of knowledge, faith, and creativity—a sanctuary where humanity's highest artistic expressions converge under the auspices of the Holy See.

Spanning over 7 kilometers (4.3 miles) of corridors and galleries, with more than 70,000 works of art (of which about 20,000 are on display), the Vatican Museums house the greatest private art collection in the world, curated by popes over centuries to reflect not just wealth or power but divine beauty and universal truth.

At the heart of it all lies the Sistine Chapel, where Michelangelo's ceiling and Last Judgment remain perhaps the most sublime marriage of art and theology ever produced. To walk beneath them is to feel suspended between time and eternity.

A Brief History of the Vatican Museums
The story of the Vatican Museums begins with Pope Julius II in the early 16th century. A warrior pope and Renaissance patron, Julius II commissioned Donato Bramante to redesign St. Peter's Basilica and recruited Michelangelo and Raphael to adorn the Vatican Palace. But his greatest cultural act may have been placing the Laocoön Group—a Hellenistic marble sculpture unearthed in 1506—on public display in the Belvedere Courtyard.

This event marked the birth of the Vatican Museums, which over the next 500 years would grow to include art from ancient Egypt, Greece, Rome, the Renaissance, the Baroque era, and beyond.

Each successive pope contributed to the collection, driven by a mix of personal taste, religious ideology, political strategy, and a deep belief in the civilizing force of art.

Navigating the Vatican Museums
Visiting the Vatican Museums is not a passive stroll. It's a pilgrimage through art history, a test of your stamina, your eyes, and your soul. You will encounter rooms filled with:

Ancient sculptures,

Renaissance frescoes,

Tapestries, maps, papal treasures,

Contemporary religious art,

And corridors that seem to stretch infinitely.

The full museum experience typically takes 3 to 5 hours, though many spend an entire day trying to absorb the richness of the collection.

Practical Advice:
Arrive early—crowds are immense even in low season.

Pre-book tickets online to skip the long queues.

Wear comfortable shoes—you'll walk miles.

Use a guide or audio guide—context enhances everything.

Stay hydrated, and don't try to "see it all"—focus on the highlights that speak to you.

The Highlights of the Vatican Museums
Let us now walk, room by room, through the key areas of the Vatican Museums.

The Pinecone Courtyard (Cortile della Pigna)
You enter the Vatican Museums through the Cortile della Pigna, named after a massive bronze pinecone (nearly 4 meters high) that once adorned a Roman fountain. This ancient pagan symbol of eternal life and regeneration now welcomes pilgrims into the sacred halls.

Also featured is the Sphere Within a Sphere (Sfera con Sfera) sculpture by Arnaldo Pomodoro, a modern masterpiece that represents the fragility and interconnectedness of the world.

Pio-Clementine Museum
Established by Popes Clement XIV and Pius VI in the late 1700s, this section features:

The Laocoön Group, a dramatic marble sculpture of the Trojan priest and his sons attacked by sea serpents—widely considered a Hellenistic masterpiece.

The Apollo Belvedere, the epitome of idealized male beauty.

The Belvedere Torso, a fragment that inspired Michelangelo's muscular style.

These sculptures bridge pagan antiquity and Christian aesthetics, reinforcing the idea that beauty is a pathway to divine truth.

Gallery of the Candelabra, Tapestries, and Maps
These three grand galleries are architectural marvels:

Gallery of the Candelabra
Features ancient Roman sculptures, colossal marble candelabras, and sarcophagi of pagan and early Christian origin.

It's a fusion of light, form, and ritual.

Gallery of the Tapestries
Houses Flemish tapestries made by students of Raphael, depicting the life of Christ and the apostles.

Observe the illusionistic detail—Christ's eyes seem to follow you.

Gallery of the Maps
Commissioned by Pope Gregory XIII in the 16th century.

Contains 40 painted topographical maps of Italy, painted in brilliant greens and blues.

These maps are not just cartographic—they're theological, expressing divine order through geography.

Raphael Rooms (Stanze di Raffaello)
The Raphael Rooms are four papal apartments frescoed by Raphael and his students, commissioned by Pope Julius II as his personal residence.

The School of Athens (Stanza della Segnatura)
Raphael's magnum opus.

Depicts Plato, Aristotle, Socrates, Pythagoras, Euclid, and other classical thinkers.

Leonardo da Vinci appears as Plato, while Michelangelo is portrayed brooding in the foreground.

It's a visual manifesto of Renaissance humanism.

Other rooms include:

Stanza di Eliodoro (Heliodorus Driven from the Temple): Symbolizes divine protection of the Church.

Stanza dell'Incendio del Borgo: Papal miracles through history.

Sala di Costantino: Features Constantine's vision and victory.

The Borgia Apartments
Decorated by Pinturicchio in the 1490s, these rooms once housed Pope Alexander VI—the infamous Rodrigo Borgia. The art is stunning, but many visitors find equal intrigue in the stories of papal decadence, intrigue, and power that hover in the air.

Modern Religious Art Collection
Often overlooked, this section includes works by

Salvador Dalí,

Vincent van Gogh,

Marc Chagall,

Francis Bacon,

Giorgio de Chirico.

It proves that spirituality is not confined to the Renaissance—modernity also seeks God in bold, fractured, existential ways.

The Sistine Chapel
No matter how long you've spent in the Vatican Museums, nothing prepares you for the awe of entering the Sistine Chapel.

Built between 1473 and 1481 under Pope Sixtus IV, the chapel was meant to house papal ceremonies and conclaves—the election of new popes. But its destiny changed forever when Michelangelo painted the ceiling between 1508 and 1512

Historical Context
Commissioned by Pope Sixtus IV in 1473 (from whom it takes its name), the Sistine Chapel was originally intended as a private chapel for papal services and an official space for conclaves, the sacred gatherings where new popes are elected.

Its architectural design by Giovanni dei Dolci follows the proportions of Solomon's Temple as described in the Old Testament, symbolizing continuity with divine authority.

While several prominent Renaissance artists—Botticelli, Ghirlandaio, Perugino, and Rosselli—were called to fresco the lower walls with biblical scenes from the lives of Moses and Christ, the chapel as we know it today owes its legendary status to Michelangelo Buonarroti.

Michelangelo's Ceiling (1508–1512)
A Reluctant Genius
When Pope Julius II ordered Michelangelo to paint the ceiling of the Sistine Chapel in 1508, the sculptor initially resisted. He considered himself a sculptor, not a painter, and resented the politics of the papal court.

Yet over four years, lying on his back atop scaffolding he built himself, Michelangelo produced a work that redefined not just Renaissance art but the limits of human imagination.

The Visual Program
The ceiling spans approximately 500 square meters and consists of over 300 figures. The central panels depict nine scenes from the Book of Genesis, from the Separation of Light from Darkness to the Drunkenness of Noah. These scenes are framed by prophets, sibyls, ignudi (nude youths), and ancestral figures of Christ.

Iconic Scenes
Creation of Adam
Perhaps the most famous fresco in the world.

God reaches toward Adam with outstretched fingers, imparting the spark of life.

The near-touch between divine and human fingers symbolizes the moment of consciousness, the gift of intellect and spirit.

The Fall and Expulsion
A dual scene: on the left, Eve takes the apple; on the right, Adam and Eve are driven from Paradise.

The transition from innocence to shame, from divine intimacy to mortal struggle, is heartbreakingly captured.

The Deluge
A dynamic, chaotic rendering of Noah's Flood, where humanity's sin leads to its near-eradication.

The composition is claustrophobic, dramatic, and despairing—a reminder of moral responsibility.

The Ignudi
Michelangelo inserted twenty athletic male nudes—the ignudi—framing each scene.

These figures serve no explicit biblical function but elevate the work to a celebration of the ideal human form—a bridge between classical beauty and divine glory.

The Last Judgment (1536–1541)
Twenty years after painting the ceiling, Michelangelo was summoned by Pope Paul III to return and paint the altar wall of the Sistine Chapel. By this time, the Reformation was tearing Christendom apart, and Michelangelo—older and more spiritually tormented—responded with a terrifying vision of judgment and salvation.

Overview
Covering the entire wall behind the altar, The Last Judgment depicts the Second Coming of Christ and the final judgment of all souls. At its center, a muscular, stern Christ raises his hand in judgment, surrounded by saints, martyrs, and the elect rising to heaven on one side while the damned tumble into hell on the other.

Symbolism and Drama
Saint Bartholomew holds his flayed skin—his face is a self-portrait of Michelangelo, a symbol of artistic and spiritual anguish.

Charon, the Greek ferryman of the dead, is depicted ferrying souls to the underworld—a controversial pagan reference that Michelangelo used to show the universality of judgment.

The nude bodies scandalized many, and more enormous fig leaves were added by Daniele da Volterra, earning him the nickname Il Braghettone ("the breeches painter").

This work is darker, more expressionistic, and more apocalyptic than the ceiling. It reflects Michelangelo's inner turmoil and the existential anxiety of the Church in crisis.

Papal Conclaves
Beyond its artistic treasures, the Sistine Chapel is the sacred site where papal conclaves take place.

The Ritual
When a pope dies or resigns, the College of Cardinals (currently about 120 members under the age of 80) gathers in the Sistine Chapel to elect the next leader of the Catholic Church.

The voting process is conducted in secrecy.

After each vote, the ballots are burned in a special stove.

If no pope is elected, black smoke appears from the chapel's chimney.

When a new pope is chosen, white smoke signals to the world, "Habemus Papam"—"We have a pope."

Being inside the Sistine Chapel during a conclave is akin to standing inside history itself, as the continuity of papal succession plays out beneath Michelangelo's monumental warnings and promises.

Reflections
No photograph, film, or book can replicate the emotional and spiritual impact of standing beneath Michelangelo's ceiling or before his Last Judgment. The Sistine Chapel is not merely a triumph of human skill; it is a threshold between the earthly and the eternal.

Visitors often report a sense of transcendence, a quieting of the soul, or an overwhelming confrontation with human destiny—life, sin, death, and salvation—rendered in color, muscle, and divine geometry.

Visiting Tips and Insider Advice
Best Time to Visit:

Tuesdays and Thursdays tend to be less crowded.

Visit during the early morning skip-the-line tours or evening openings (April to October).

Dress Code:

Modest attire is required—no shorts, sleeveless tops, or miniskirts.

Photography:

Strictly prohibited in the Sistine Chapel.

Guided Tours:

Private tours or expert guides are recommended to fully appreciate the art, history, and symbolism.

Exit Strategy:

Most visitors exit into the Vatican Museum courtyard, but private tour groups often exit directly into St. Peter's Basilica, saving a 15-minute walk around Vatican walls.

CHAPTER 7:

SHOPPING IN ROME

Shopping in Rome is not merely a transaction; it is an encounter with style, tradition, and expression. From the grand boulevards lined with designer boutiques to the quiet alleyways hiding artisan workshops, the Eternal City offers an experience where retail becomes ritual and fashion dances with history.

This chapter explores every corner of Rome's shopping world—its glitzy fashion districts, open-air markets, handcrafted treasures, gourmet shops, and hidden gems—guiding you through a city that has dressed emperors, popes, and fashionistas alike for over two millennia.

Via dei Condotti and Rome's Luxury District:
The Golden Triangle of Roman Fashion

At the base of the Spanish Steps lies Via dei Condotti, the most prestigious and elegant shopping street in Rome. This narrow yet radiant boulevard houses the flagship stores of global fashion houses, from Gucci and Fendi to Prada, Cartier, and Hermès.

Together with Via Borgognona and Via Frattina, Via dei Condotti forms Rome's "Golden Triangle," a high-end shopping district where couture meets centuries of Roman splendor. Inside these boutiques, you'll find not only the latest seasonal collections but also private salons, personal shoppers, and custom tailoring—service elevated to ritual.

Window-Shopping as Spectacle

Even if you're not planning to splurge, walking through this area is a visual delight. The ornate window displays, set in baroque facades, present fashion as artwork in a living museum. And with the Trinità dei Monti staircase rising above and Piazza di Spagna below, the setting is nothing short of cinematic.

Via del Corso and Popular Brands
Accessible Fashion and Bustling Crowds

For a more budget-conscious shopping spree, Via del Corso offers an energetic, crowded, and youthful vibe. Stretching from Piazza Venezia to Piazza del Popolo, this long commercial artery is packed with:

Zara, H&M, Mango, and other global high-street brands

Footwear and accessory shops

Affordable Italian chains like OVS, Calzedonia, and Intimissimi

Here, teenagers, tourists, and locals rub shoulders in search of everyday fashion and seasonal bargains. It's the pulse of Rome's middle-tier retail life.

Side Streets with Surprises
Venture into the vicoli—small alleys branching off Via del Corso—and you'll find independent fashion boutiques, gelaterias, and even the occasional bespoke tailor or leather artisan tucked into a 17th-century stone shop.

Campo Marzio, Monti, and Trastevere: Artisan Rome
Campo Marzio
A short stroll from Piazza Navona lies Campo Marzio, a stylish neighborhood where Roman elegance is on full display. Here, boutiques like Gente Roma and Borsalino offer curated selections of Italian design, while concept stores fuse fashion, art, and home decor.

Monti
Monti is Rome's hipster heart—a bohemian neighborhood near the Colosseum, packed with indie labels, vintage shops, and custom denim makers. Don't miss:

Pifebo—a funky vintage store with leather jackets, retro eyewear, and vinyl records.

Le Gallinelle—avant-garde designs made in Rome.

Mercato Monti—a weekend urban market for handmade jewelry, clothing, and design objects.

Monti's boutiques emphasize individuality over labels, perfect for travelers seeking something truly Roman and truly unique.

Trastevere
Cross the Tiber to Trastevere, and you'll find craftsmanship rooted in history. From tiny workshops producing custom sandals and belts to artists creating handmade journals and mosaic tiles, this is where ancient skills survive the modern age.

Highlights include:

Polvere di Tempo—specializing in sundials, compasses, and timepieces.

La Sella—exquisite handmade leather bags.

Bookbinders and calligraphers are still practicing their art near Santa Maria in Trastevere.

Markets and Street Bazaars
Porta Portese
Every Sunday morning, Porta Portese explodes into life as Rome's largest flea market. It stretches for blocks with stalls selling:

Vintage clothes and accessories

Old postcards and records

Bicycles, military jackets, lamps, and antique furniture

Prices are negotiable, and while you must keep an eye on your belongings, bargain hunters and collectors will find it a thrilling adventure.

Campo de' Fiori and Mercato Testaccio
If your idea of shopping leans toward the edible, head to:

Campo de' Fiori: A historical square where produce stalls, spices, olive oil, pasta, and local liqueurs tempt your senses.

Mercato Testaccio: A modern, locals-only market offering meats, cheeses, baked goods, and household items. Some stands also sell shoes, dresses, and bags—often at better prices than tourist zones.

Roman Specialties
Leather Goods
Rome has long been known for exquisite leather products, rivaling even Florence. Seek out:

Sermoneta Gloves—handcrafted Italian gloves in rainbow hues.

Il Bisonte – rustic luxury bags and belts.

Del Giudice Roma—known for hand-sewn, timeless designs.

Jewelry and Goldsmiths
Italy's goldsmith tradition shines in Rome. Visit Via dell'Orso or Via Margutta to find:

Handmade rings and necklaces

Cameos and coral jewelry

Family-run shops with multi-generational craftsmanship

Paper Goods and Stationery
From hand-marbled paper to leather-bound journals, Rome's papeterie shops make perfect souvenirs. Try:

Il Papiro

Fabriano Boutique

Cartoleria Pantheon

Shopping Tips, Etiquette, and Practicalities
Sales Seasons
Winter sales begin in early January and last through February.

Summer sales start in July and end by August.

During these periods, even luxury shops offer significant discounts—but go early for the best picks.

VAT Refunds for Non-EU Visitors
If you spend over €154.94 in a single store, you may be eligible for a VAT (IVA) refund of 12–15%.

Ask for a tax-free form at the time of purchase.

Present it at the airport customs desk when departing the EU.

Opening Hours and Siesta Culture
Most shops open around 10:00 AM and close at 7:30 PM.

Independent stores may close for lunch (1–4 PM) and on Sundays.

Malls and chains on Via del Corso usually stay open straight through.

Sustainable and Ethical Shopping
Rome is also embracing slow fashion, with brands prioritizing sustainability, fair labor, and organic materials. Look for:

Eco-à-Porter in Monti

Re(f)use Roma – upcycled accessories from recycled materials

Neomatique – handbags from bicycle inner tubes

Buying from these shops is not only stylish but also ethical and environmentally conscious.

Shopping as Cultural Immersion
Shopping in Rome isn't just commerce. It's contact with identity, dialogue with artisans, and participation in an age-old continuum of trade, beauty, and craftsmanship.

Whether you leave with a pair of designer shoes, a handmade ceramic, or a simple bar of olive oil soap, what you're really taking home is a fragment of Roman soul—shaped by the hands of its creators, wrapped in centuries of tradition, and infused with the eternal charm of the city itself.

CHAPTER 8:

ROMAN NIGHTLIFE

Few cities reinvent themselves with the falling of the sun like Rome. If the city by day is a living museum, the city by night is poetry written in light and shadow. It is a Rome less concerned with history books and more in love with living well. Night in Rome is not a respite from the day's adventures—it is a continuation of the Roman rhythm, a time to indulge, connect, and discover.

Rome doesn't sleep early. It doesn't shout to be heard. Instead, its nightlife gently seduces with whispers through illuminated alleyways, soft laughter echoing across centuries-old stones, and music wafting through wooden shutters. As you venture into the Roman evening, you become not just a tourist but a participant in a millennia-old ritual: to live well, love deeply, eat slowly, and savor every moment.

A Brief History of Roman Nights
Ancient Nights

In Ancient Rome, nightlife was a spectacle. The Romans were not shy about indulgence. Elite Roman society engaged in convivia—lavish evening banquets that began with wine and ended with entertainment ranging from philosophy to poetry to acrobatics and even sensual pleasures.

Public spaces like the Forum Romanum and Campo Marzio saw activity deep into the night, especially during festivals such as Saturnalia or Bacchanalia, which turned Rome into a swirling celebration of wine, music, and dance. Torchlit processions, open-air performances, and public feasting defined the rhythm of a Roman night.

While nightlife as we know it today didn't exist in the same way, the Roman love for nocturnal living—and for celebrating under the stars—dates back over two thousand years.

Medieval to Renaissance Nights

During the Middle Ages, much of Rome slept with the sun. With poor lighting and lawlessness after dark, venturing out at night was rare. Still, candlelit taverns and noble palazzos would host gatherings, often revolving around faith, food, or forbidden pleasures. By the Renaissance, the tide turned again—Rome reembraced the night, with art salons, musical gatherings, and open-air celebrations, especially in noble villas and Vatican courts.

Understanding Modern Roman Nightlife Culture
To understand nightlife in Rome, you must first understand Romans themselves. They live life passionately, with unforced style and ritual. Their nights are unhurried. They stroll before they drink, laugh before they eat, and always, always talk. A night out is not a checklist of venues—it's a flow of experiences, where where you go is secondary to whom you're with and how you live the moment.

Unlike other European capitals, Rome's nightlife is more about atmosphere than excess. You'll find few places open at 4 AM, and clubs rarely throb with chaos. Instead, there's music that invites, not overwhelms; conversations that matter; and nights that end under the stars, gelato in hand.

Aperitivo and Golden Hour
Aperitivo as Cultural Ceremony
Aperitivo isn't simply a pre-dinner drink—it's a social ritual, a way to say, "The day is done, and now we relax." Roman locals will gather at corner cafés, terrace bars, or elegant lounges with friends or lovers, enjoying drinks that balance bitterness and refreshment: a Negroni, a Hugo, or a Spritz. The food is not just snacks—it's miniature culinary art, often complimentary.

Venues like:

Ginger Sapori e Salute (Via Borgognona): Fresh, trendy, and healthy.

Il Marchese (Via di Ripetta): A rare Amaro bar with over 500 liqueurs.

La Zanzara (near Vatican): Classy yet relaxed.

Sunset Spots Worth the Climb
Golden hour in Rome is not just about cocktails. Locals climb:

Gianicolo Hill: For sunsets above Trastevere.

Pincian Terrace (Pincio): Above Piazza del Popolo, perfect for romance.

Aventine Keyhole: For the thrill of spying the dome of St. Peter's perfectly framed through the Knights of Malta gate.

The Neighborhoods of Roman Nightlife
Trastevere

Trastevere is Rome's most beloved nightlife quarter. Its cobblestone alleys, glowing lanterns, and tumbling ivy-covered walls create an atmosphere of romance and discovery. Live music floats from doorways, and every trattoria spills with stories.

Highlights:

Freni e Frizioni: Aperitivo heaven.

Bar San Calisto: Local dive with a loyal following.

Pimm's Good: Casual with international flair.

Wander through Piazza Santa Maria in Trastevere, where artists sketch by starlight and violins serenade late diners.

Monti

By day, Monti is vintage shops and espresso bars. By night, it becomes a low-key lounge district where Romans go to avoid crowds.

Top Night Stops:

Blackmarket Hall: Dark, moody, stylish cocktails.

Ai Tre Scalini: A rustic wine bar set in a 19th-century apothecary.

Barzilai: Quiet, intimate, and perfect for couples.

Campo de' Fiori and Piazza Navona

Campo de' Fiori is for the young and energetic. Expect Irish pubs, hookah bars, and late-night revelry. It's loud, chaotic, and full of life.

Piazza Navona, by contrast, is majestic—ideal for a quieter evening. Sit at an outdoor table, order a digestivo, and listen to the trickling of Bernini's fountains.

Testaccio

Locals head to Testaccio—gritty, passionate, and pulsing with authenticity. Once home to Rome's slaughterhouses, it's now the city's music and clubbing capital.

Club Highlights:

Akab: Diverse music, retro style.

Piper Club: A historic venue with 1960s heritage.

Coyote: Latin beats and student crowds.

Speakeasies, Enotecas, and Craft Cocktail Artistry
Hidden Treasures
Rome's speakeasy culture has blossomed. Behind anonymous doors and whispered codes lie world-class cocktail temples.

The Jerry Thomas Project: Password-protected, reservations required.

Spirito: Hidden behind a retro deli.

Club Derrière: A Parisian-inspired hideaway with velvet charm.

Each bar is not just a place to drink—it's a performance, where bartenders are mixologists and every cocktail tells a story.

Wine Lovers' Paradise
Rome's enoteca culture is thriving. Whether you're sipping rare Barolo in a vaulted cellar or enjoying bubbly Franciacorta under the stars, wine is central to Roman evenings.

Il Goccetto: Over 800 labels in a medieval setting.

Enoteca Cavour 313: Classic and cozy.

Bulzoni: A wine shop, bar, and osteria all in one.

Music, Culture, and Performance After Dark
Jazz and Live Music
Rome boasts a thriving jazz and indie music scene.

Alexanderplatz: Rome's oldest jazz club.

Charity Café: Blues and soul in Monti.

Big Mama: Intimate, legendary, and electric.

Nighttime Theatre and Opera
In summer, attend open-air opera at the Baths of Caracalla, where arias echo through ancient ruins. Year-round, enjoy:

Teatro dell'Opera di Roma

Auditorium Parco della Musica

Cinema Under the Stars
From rooftop cinemas in Trastevere to temporary screens in Villa Borghese, Rome offers outdoor film nights, often featuring Italian classics subtitled in English.

Rome by Foot at Night
Night is the perfect time to rediscover Rome by foot. The city's marble and travertine glow under amber lamplight, and each monument seems to breathe.

The Spanish Steps after midnight: intimate and echoing with history.

The Pantheon at 2 AM: Haunting and still.

The Roman Forum from Via dei Fori Imperiali: Floodlit ruins stretching to the Colosseum.

Couples stroll arm in arm. Solo travelers sit beside fountains. Groups burst into song. This is Rome at her most timeless and tender.

Street Food, Gelato, and Midnight Indulgence
The Sweet Side of the Night
Late-night gelato is an art form. Romans queue up at:

Gelateria del Teatro

Frigidarium

Come il Latte

Midnight Pizza and Suppli Runs
Street food never sleeps. In Trastevere and Prati, you'll find:

Supplizio: High-end street food.

La Renella: Bakery pumping out hot bread till 2 AM.

Pizza Zazà: Simple slices with explosive flavor.

Seasonal Nightlife
Summer: Outdoor concerts, rooftop parties, riverbank festivals, and piazza picnics.

Winter: Warm wine bars, candlelit taverns, underground music.

Each season shifts the flavor of nightlife, but the vibe remains constant—intimate, open, and full of humanity.

Safety, Navigation, and Etiquette
Taxis can be hailed via app (FreeNow, IT Taxi).

Walk with awareness—petty theft exists, especially near Termini.

Dress the part—Romans care about la bella figura (the beautiful appearance).

Public transport ends by 12:30 AM, so plan accordingly.

CHAPTER 9:

ROMAN CUISINE

The Foundations of Roman Cuisine: Simplicity, Soul, and Season
The Roman Philosophy
Roman cuisine is built not on extravagance, but on elegant simplicity. The key elements are few: pecorino cheese, guanciale, olive oil, fresh eggs, tomatoes, artichokes, wild herbs, white wine, and offal. What elevates them is technique, time, and tradition.

Unlike the butter-laden dishes of northern Italy or the seafood-rich feasts of the south, Rome's cooking reflects its agrarian past and deeply rooted peasant traditions. It's humble. Honest. And unforgettable.

Seasonality is Sacred
Romans eat with the seasons, not against them. You'll find artichokes in spring, figs in summer, truffles in autumn, and chestnuts in winter. The idea of eating strawberries in December is not just odd—it's sacrilege.

In Rome, what you eat is when you eat.

Rome's Quintessential Pasta Dishes
Rome is the pasta capital of the world, and four iconic dishes define its culinary DNA. If you understand these, you understand Roman flavor.

Cacio e Pepe (Cheese and Pepper)
Ingredients: Pecorino Romano, black pepper, pasta (usually tonnarelli or spaghetti).

Essence: Ancient simplicity. No butter. No cream. Just three ingredients that, when emulsified properly, create one of the most decadent sauces imaginable.

This dish is Rome stripped bare, and all the more powerful for it.

Amatriciana
Ingredients: Guanciale (cured pork), pecorino, tomato, white wine, chili.

History: Originated in Amatrice, a town near Rome, and adopted fiercely by Romans. It's fiery, rich, and smoky.

Carbonara

Ingredients: Guanciale, egg yolks, pecorino, black pepper, pasta.

Myth Busting: No cream. Ever. Cream in carbonara is an insult to every Roman nonna who's ever stirred a pot.

Carbonara is Rome's love letter to indulgence, and when done right, it borders on the sublime.

Gricia
Ingredients: Guanciale, pecorino, and black pepper.

Known As: The "white Amatriciana"—a dish so old it predates tomatoes in Europe.

Gricia is the forgotten hero of Roman pasta, rich in umami, deceptively simple.

Antipasti
Antipasti in Rome is not just about whetting the appetite—it's a chance to honor small bites with big stories.

Supplì (Roman Rice Balls)
A crispy, fried ball of risotto with ragù and mozzarella, named "supplì al telefono" because the melted cheese stretches like a phone cord.

Where to try:

Supplizio (Via dei Banchi Vecchi): Gourmet versions by renowned chef Arcangelo Dandini.

La Casa del Supplì (Trastevere): Classic Roman.

Carciofi alla Giudia (Jewish-style Artichokes)
Deep-fried until golden and crispy, this iconic dish comes from the Jewish Ghetto, dating back to the 16th century. A perfect blend of history and crunch.

Fiori di Zucca (Zucchini Flowers)
Stuffed with mozzarella and anchovies, dipped in batter, and fried. Ephemeral and delicate, available only in summer.

Secondi

Secondi courses showcase Rome's rustic heart. Forget steak or fancy fillets. Rome is about slow-cooked, earthy, deeply flavored dishes, often featuring cuts others ignore.

Saltimbocca alla Romana
Thin veal slices, prosciutto, sage, white wine, and butter. The name means "jumps in the mouth," and it does.

Abbacchio (Roast Lamb)
Spring lamb seasoned with rosemary, garlic, and vinegar. A traditional Easter dish that fills homes with joy.

Trippa alla Romana (Tripe)
Braised cow's stomach in tomato sauce and mint, topped with pecorino. Not for the faint-hearted, but a delicacy for the brave.

Contorni and Insalate: Sides with Meaning
Contorni (vegetable sides) in Rome aren't afterthoughts. They are expressions of the land.

Puntarelle
Chicory shoots, finely cut and dressed in anchovy vinaigrette. Only in winter.

Cicoria Ripassata
Sautéed chicory with garlic and chili. Bitter, bold, and addictive.

Dolce Vita
Tiramisu
Though invented in the north, Rome perfected it.

Maritozzo
A sweet yeast bun, sliced and stuffed with whipped cream. Once gifted by Roman lovers in Lent.

Crostata di Visciole
A cherry tart with ricotta, traditionally made in the Jewish Ghetto. Sweet, tart, and spiritual.

Roman Street Food
Rome's street food is alive and delicious. Stand on a cobbled corner, lean against a wall, and devour:

Pizza al taglio: Cut pizza sold by weight. Try it at Bonci Pizzarium near the Vatican.

Trapizzino: A modern invention—pizza dough pockets filled with Roman stews.

Porchetta Panini: Roast pork sandwiches seasoned with fennel and garlic.

Markets
Campo de' Fiori
The most famous, selling produce since the 1800s.

Mercato Testaccio
Where locals shop for real food. Raw, authentic, and proud.

Mercato di Campagna Amica
Farmers' market near Circo Massimo, offering organic meats, cheeses, wines, and oils.

The Roman Table
Dinner starts late—8 PM at the earliest.

Don't rush. Meals are events.

Bread is not served with olive oil.

Water and wine are standard. Don't ask for soda with pasta.

Tipping is minimal—but gratitude is always welcome.

Where to Eat
Historic Institutions
Armando al Pantheon: Traditional excellence.

Checchino dal 1887 (Testaccio): Fifth-generation offal mastery.

La Campana: oldest restaurant in Rome (since 1518).
Campana: The
Modern Stars
Roscioli: Charcuterie, wine, pasta—gourmet heaven.

Retrobottega: Inventive, intimate, unforgettable.

Pipero: Michelin-starred carbonara.

Food Experiences
Cooking classes in Trastevere or Testaccio.

Food tours through Campo de' Fiori.

Olive oil tastings and cheese workshops in enotecas.

Vineyard day trips to Frascati or Castelli Romani.

Seasonal and Festive Foods
Carnevale: Eat frappe and castagnole.

Easter: Try abaccio and pizza pasquale.

Christmas: Pangiallo and panettone dominate.

The Roman Breakfast
Many visitors arrive in Rome expecting a hearty breakfast—eggs, bacon, toast—but the Roman morning is far more restrained and elegant.

What Do Romans Really Eat for Breakfast?
Cornetto e Caffè: The classic combo. A flaky, crescent-shaped pastry often filled with marmalade, chocolate, or custard, paired with a cappuccino (never after 11 a.m.).

Caffè Macchiato or Espresso: Sipped while standing at the bar, served quickly, meant to energize—not linger over.

Best Places for a Roman Breakfast Experience
Sant'Eustachio Il Caffè (near the Pantheon): Rome's legendary coffeehouse with secret roasting techniques.

Pasticceria Regoli (Esquilino): A 100-year-old pastry shop famous for cream-filled maritozzi and fluffy crostate.

Panella – L'Arte del Pane: A breakfast institution known for Roman breads and creative morning pastries.

Rome's Enoteca and Aperitivo Culture
What is aperitivo?
Aperitivo is not just a drink—it's a social hour, a cultural pause before dinner where Romans gather to unwind.

Typical Aperitivo Items
Small plates: olives, cheeses, salumi, and bruschetta.

Drinks: Spritz, Negroni, prosecco, or regional wines.

Where to Go for Aperitivo
Il Goccetto (Via dei Banchi Vecchi): A cozy enoteca with hundreds of wines by the glass.

Freni e Frizioni (Trastevere): Popular with locals, this former mechanic shop turned bar offers generous aperitivo spreads.

Salotto 42 (Piazza di Pietra): Chic, artsy lounge with a stylish clientele and craft cocktails.

Exploring Rome's Culinary Neighborhoods
Rome isn't just one food culture—it's a mosaic of local micro-scenes. Each neighborhood offers its own flavors, pace, and culinary philosophy.

Trastevere
Known for its cobbled lanes and romantic trattorias.

Great for rustic Roman dishes, homemade pasta, and vibrant piazza dining.

Testaccio
The true culinary soul of Rome.

Birthplace of Roman offal cuisine.

Visit Flavio al Velavevodetto for pasta and Trapizzino for street food innovation.

Campo de' Fiori
Market by day, buzzing wine bars by night.

Try Forno Campo de' Fiori for pizza bianca and fresh focaccia.

Monti
Creative, stylish, and locally driven.

Small bistros and wine shops with modern takes on tradition.

Ai Tre Scalini is beloved for natural wines and small plates.

Food and Religion
Vatican Cuisine
The Vatican has its own culinary culture:

Swiss Guard favorites like rösti and beer.

Vatican Cafeteria (yes, tourists can dine there on some tours).

Jewish-Roman Cuisine
Originated in the Ghetto di Roma, dating back to 1555.

Key Dishes: Carciofi alla Giudia, Concia di Zucchine (marinated zucchini), and Torta di Ricotta.

Visit Nonna Betta or Sora Margherita for an unforgettable meal rooted in tradition and resilience.

Roman Beverages
Coffee Culture
Don't order cappuccino in the afternoon—it's considered childish.

Stand at the bar for a quick espresso like a local.

Tip: Avoid sitting down at tourist cafés; it adds a coperto (table charge).

Wines of Lazio
Frascati: Light white wine from the Castelli Romani hills.

Cesanese: A robust red gaining gourmet recognition.

Wine is meant to complement food, not dominate the table.

Digestivi and Amari
After meals, Romans often sip:

Limoncello (Amalfi lemon liqueur)

Amaro Montenegro, Fernet, or Cynar—bitters that aid digestion.

Special Diets in Rome
Vegetarians and Vegans
Try: Zucchine alla scapece, Puntarelle, Fiori di zucca, Caponata, and more.

Rifugio Romano and Ecru are highly rated vegan spots.

Gluten-Free Travelers
Gluten-free pizza, pasta, and even tiramisu can be found.

Mama Eat and La Soffitta Renovatio are certified by the Italian Celiac Association.

Food-Related Day Trips from Rome
Frascati (30 minutes from Termini Station)
Famed for white wine, vineyards, and countryside feasts.

Visit wine estates like Cantine Santa Benedetta for tastings.

Castelli Romani
A cluster of villages including Ariccia (for porchetta) and Grottaferrata (for rustic cuisine).

Best enjoyed on a Sunday when Romans escape the city for a lazy lunch in the hills.

The Roman Kitchen
Best Cooking Classes in Rome
Cooking Classes in Rome (Trastevere): Small-group pasta and tiramisu making.

Eataly Rome: Offers professional courses for more advanced enthusiasts.

Pasta e Basta: Make tagliatelle, gnocchi, and sauces from scratch with local chefs.

Visit a Roman Food Lab
Join pasta-making experiences in Testaccio.

Learn about cheese aging, gelato creation, or bread baking.

Rome's Culinary Superstitions and Sayings
Romans are a superstitious people—and the kitchen is no exception.

"Chi magna bene, vive bene"—Who eats well, lives well.

Never cross knives on a plate—it's bad luck.

Don't flip fish—turning over a fish is said to sink the boat.

Always toast eye-to-eye—or risk seven years of bad sex (yes, really).

Recipes Passed Down Generations (Optional Page Inserts)
Would you like to include handwritten-style recipes, styled as family heirlooms? Some suggestions:

Tonnarelli Cacio e Pepe

Carciofi alla Romana

Roman Semolina Gnocchi (Gnocchi alla Romana)

Each could be formatted like a scrapbook note, giving your book texture and intimacy.

CHAPTER 10:

ROME FOR FAMILIES

1. Why Rome Is a Great Family Destination
At first glance, Rome might appear too sophisticated or chaotic for families with children. Yet few cities manage to balance ancient history, modern convenience, and family-friendly charm as effortlessly as the Eternal City. Rome is not only a living museum; it's a hands-on classroom, a flavorful feast, and an open-air playground. Kids don't just learn—they live history here.

Why It Works:
The History Is Alive: Rome's ruins aren't locked behind glass; you can walk through them, touch ancient stones, and see gladiator schools in person.

Open Spaces for Exploration: Piazzas, parks, and fountains invite running, laughing, and ice cream-eating—without fear of disturbing others.

Food They'll Love: Pizza. Pasta. Gelato. Repeat.

Locals Love Children: Romans are famously family-oriented, and children are welcome almost everywhere.

Hands-On Learning: History, art, language, and food become exciting adventures for young travelers.

Rome isn't just a city for the seasoned traveler—it's an interactive storybook for families.

2. Planning a Family-Friendly Roman Holiday
Success starts with planning. Families need to consider:

Pace

Location

Interests by age

Downtime

Emergency access

Accessibility

When to Go with Kids
Spring (April–June) and Fall (late September–October) are ideal. Not too hot, not too crowded.

Avoid peak summer: July and August can be punishing with temperatures above 35°C (95°F).

How Long to Stay
3–5 days minimum for younger children.

7–10 days allows for relaxed pacing and side trips.

Booking Tips
Book skip-the-line tickets to all attractions.

Reserve family-friendly accommodations early.

Look for hotels or rentals with kitchens, lifts, and laundry facilities.

Must-Pack Items
Sunscreen and hats

Refillable water bottles (Rome has over 1,500 public fountains!)

Lightweight stroller

Baby carrier for cobblestone-heavy areas

Wet wipes and snacks

3. Where to Stay with Kids—Family-Oriented Accommodations
Not all areas in Rome are equally suited for families. Choose based on walkability, amenities, and proximity to parks or attractions.

Top Neighborhoods for Families:
Prati: Calm, elegant, near the Vatican, and spacious sidewalks.

Monti: Centrally located, full of charm and small piazzas.

Trastevere: Atmospheric, slightly bohemian, full of trattorias, and easy to walk.

Aventine Hill: Quiet, residential, leafy, and beautiful.

Accommodation Types:
Apartments or Vacation Rentals: Ideal for longer stays. Kitchen, privacy, more space.

Family Suites in Hotels: Book hotels with cribs, kids' breakfast options, and adjacent rooms.

Agriturismo near Rome: For rural tranquility, some farms near Rome offer family stays with fresh food and nature experiences.

Kid-Friendly Hotel Amenities to Look For:
Baby cots or high chairs

Play areas

In-room fridge or kitchenette

Laundry access

Lift or ground floor room (avoid lugging strollers up stairs)

4. Getting Around with Children
Transportation Options
Walking: Rome is a walking city. Use carriers for infants and narrow strollers for toddlers.

Public Transit: Children under 10 ride free. Trams and buses are more stroller-friendly than the metro.

Taxis and Uber: Taxis are regulated. Uber exists but is expensive. Always request a child seat if needed.

Hop-on, Hop-off Buses: Great for tired kids and sightseeing without walking.

Car Rentals: Not recommended in central Rome unless venturing outside the city.

Stroller Tips
A lightweight, collapsible stroller is ideal.

Expect cobblestones—some areas are tough terrain.

Elevators are scarce in older buildings and metro stations.

Safety Tips
Keep children close in crowds.

Use ID bracelets or tags.

Teach basic Italian phrases like "Dov'è il bagno?" (Where is the bathroom?).

5. Top Attractions for Kids
Colosseum
Gladiator tours allow kids to dress up and play Roman soldier.

Underground and arena floor access = thrilling.

Use the interactive apps to explain the amphitheater's use.

Roman Forum and Palatine Hill
Ancient temples, market ruins, and stories of emperors.

Spot wildflowers and cats among the stones.

Pantheon
Free to enter, it's awe-inspiring with its massive dome.

Talk about how it still stands after 2,000 years.

Trevi Fountain
Teach the coin toss tradition—right hand over left shoulder.

Let kids count how many coins land!

Castel Sant'Angelo

Secret passageways, towers, and views—it feels like a medieval fortress from a storybook.

6. Interactive Museums and Hands-On Learning
Explora—Il Museo dei Bambini di Roma
Rome's children's museum.

Mini supermarket, firetruck, labs, workshops.

Suited for ages 0–12.

Time Elevator Rome
5D multisensory experience through Rome's history.

Ideal for older children.

Leonardo da Vinci Experience
Hands-on models of Da Vinci's inventions.

Great for curious minds aged 7+.

Cinecittà Studios
Visit Italy's Hollywood.

Interactive film sets, costumes, and virtual tours.

Vigamus (Video Game Museum)
Arcade machines, retro games, and interactive exhibits.

Teens and tweens will love this.

ITINERARY

3-Day Family Itinerary with Kids

Day 1: Ancient Rome Comes Alive
Morning: Colosseum with kid-friendly guided tour. Book arena floor access.

Lunch: Casual pizzeria near the Forum (La Prezzemolina or Pizza Forum).

Afternoon: Roman Forum & Palatine Hill. Use storytelling to explain ruins.

Snack: Gelato at Fatamorgana Monti.

Evening: Dinner in Monti. Early bedtime or a short walk to Piazza Venezia for night lights.

Day 2: Vatican and the Tiber Walk
Morning: Vatican Museums (2 hours max with kids). Skip the Sistine Chapel if kids are very young.

Lunch: Trattoria in Prati.

Afternoon: Castel Sant'Angelo. Climb to the top. Play swordfight.

Stroll along the Tiber River.

Dinner: River-view restaurant with Roman pasta.

Day 3: Piazza Magic and Explora Museum
Morning: Piazza Navona, street artists, fountains. Visit the nearby Pantheon.

Midday: Explore the Museum (Explora) for hands-on learning.

Lunch: On-site café at the museum.

Afternoon: Spanish Steps, quick stop for photos, then shopping at nearby toy stores.

Evening: Farewell dinner in Trastevere.

5-Day Family Itinerary

Day 1–2: As Above
Day 3: Parks and Piazzas
Morning: Villa Borghese Park. Rent bikes or pedal boats.

Lunch: Picnic in the park or visit Casina di Raffaello (kids' café).

Afternoon: Bioparco Zoo or Puppet Theatre.

Evening: Casual trattoria near Piazza del Popolo.

Day 4: Time Travel and Leonardo
Morning: Time Elevator 5D Show (fun history lesson).

Late Morning: Leonardo da Vinci Museum.

Lunch: Taverna del Seminario.

Afternoon: Climb Janiculum Hill for cannon fire at noon and amazing views.

Evening: Pizza night! Try Bonci Pizzarium (famous Roman pizza).

Day 5: Trevi, Shopping, and Departure
Morning: Trevi Fountain, then souvenir and gelato stop.

Late morning: Visit small artisan toy shops in Campo de' Fiori.

Lunch: Light fare before transfer to airport/station.

7-Day Family Itinerary:

Days 1–5: Follow 5-Day Plan
Day 6: Day Trip to Ostia Antica
Morning–Afternoon: Take a 30-min train to Ostia Antica (like a mini Pompeii, but less crowded).

Let kids run along old Roman roads and visit baths, bakeries, and amphitheaters.

Lunch: Packed lunch or trattoria at the entrance.

Return in the afternoon.

Day 7: Treasure Hunt and Cooking
Morning: Family treasure hunt around Rome (several companies offer this).

Late morning: Family cooking class—make pasta or pizza together.

Lunch: Enjoy your creations.

Afternoon: Chill in Trastevere—stop for souvenirs, play in Piazza Santa Maria.

Evening: Grand farewell dinner. Optional gelato crawl.

Printed in Dunstable, United Kingdom